Dilemmas in
Liberal Democratic Thought
Since Max Weber

Major Concepts in Politics and Political Theory

Garrett Ward Sheldon
General Editor

Vol. 10

PETER LANG
New York • Washington, D.C./Baltimore
Bern • Frankfurt am Main • Berlin • Vienna • Paris

Richard Wellen

Dilemmas in Liberal Democratic Thought Since Max Weber

PETER LANG
New York • Washington, D.C./Baltimore
Bern • Frankfurt am Main • Berlin • Vienna • Paris

Library of Congress Cataloging-in-Publication Data

Wellen, Richard.
Dilemmas in liberal democratic thought since Max Weber/ Richard Wellen.
p. cm. — (Major concepts in politics and political theory; vol. 10)
Includes bibliographical references (p.   ) and index.
1. Liberalism. 2. Weber, Max, 1864–1920—Contributions
in political science. I. Title. II. Series.
JC574.W45   320.5'13—dc20   95-34822
ISBN 0-8204-3008-0
ISSN 1059-3535

Die Deutsche Bibliothek-CIP-Einheitsaufnahme

Wellen, Richard:
Dilemmas in liberal democratic thought since Max Weber/
Richard Wellen.–New York; Washington, D.C./Baltimore; Bern;
Frankfurt am Main; Berlin; Vienna; Paris: Lang.
(Major concepts in politics and political theory; Vol. 10)
ISBN 0-8204-3008-0
NE: GT

Cover design by James F. Brisson.

The paper in this book meets the guidelines for permanence and durability
of the Committee on Production Guidelines for Book Longevity
of the Council of Library Resources.

Printed in the United States of America.

*For Sally, Sarah
and Ruth*

Contents

Acknowledgements

The idea of addressing the relevance of Max Weber's work to contemporary political thought was suggested to me by John O'Neill during the formative stages of this project. For this, and for his patient insights into how this study could be improved in its own terms, I owe him a tremendous debt of gratitude. Tom Wilson led me to an appreciation of how Max Weber, who was a product of his times and the victim of his own ambiguous insights into the nature of intellectual and political problems, nevertheless remains a figure inviting new interpretations. I have been tremendously influenced by Brian Caterino's ambitious understanding of how both Habermas' work and contemporary debates on liberalism could be combined as a context for understanding Weber. I count myself very fortunate to have drawn so heavily from his exacting approach to the issues addressed in this study. Finally, Millie Bakan has always displayed an unflinching support for my work. I am particularly grateful for her nourishing combination of critique and conversational generosity which it has been my great fortune to enjoy for so many years.

Thanks also go to Ron Beiner for his especially close reading and valuable comments on the text. I am also grateful to York University which has generously afforded me several conference grants to present earlier versions of some of the chapters. Unfortunately, there is really no space here to acknowledge the support of so many other colleagues and friends whose imprint on my work has been worth so much more than the thanks I could ever hope to give them.

Of course, this study would not have been possible had my wife and my two children not given me the confidence that they would survive (if not always relish) the many seasons in which they were subjected to the renewal of this project.

Chapter One

WEBER'S CHALLENGE TO POLITICAL THOUGHT

Max Weber's work has become famous for its portrait of the ambiguous legacy of the forms of rationalization in religion and society, Enlightenment liberalism, modern democracy, "rational bourgeois capitalism," and the spread of objectification and depersonalization in modern spheres of conduct and organization.   However, the recent lively controversies about liberalism among political philosophers in North America have rarely spawned much sustained discussion of Weber's core themes.   This is ironic since some of the most frequently cited protagonists in these debates—primarily Leo Strauss, Jürgen Habermas and Alasdaire MacIntyre—have treated Weber as the thinker who has presented perhaps the greatest challenge to the intellectual foundations of liberalism.   It is the purpose of this study to recover Weber as a touchstone for contemporary debates in political theory.   In doing so I will usually not deal with lengthy expositions of his ideas or with a straightforward defense or criticism of his work.   Rather the hope is that I can show how the challenges Max Weber posed might help us better understand what is actually at stake in contemporary criticisms of liberalism and in recent attempts to provide it with new foundations and justifications.

WEBER AS AN AMBIGUOUS FIGURE

Donald Levine, one of the most sensitive recent interpreters of Weber's place in the sociological tradition, has shown that the keystone of

Weber's approach was to contextualize, in a careful way, the modern ideals of freedom and rationality, rather than to characterize the modern age in univocal terms as many of Weber's critics maintain.[1] Although too often theorists like Levine and Parsons 'reconstruct' Weber in ways that make his view of modern developments look rather benign, they do offer an antidote to readings that stress only Weber's statements regarding threats to freedom and the inevitability of cultural loss in the face of the increasing instrumental rationalization of life. It is clear that Weber was often centrally preoccupied with this trend which he tried to capture in his remarks about the "iron cage" of modern rationalized institutions. However, in another respect his analyses were self-consciously meant to train the eye upon selective aspects of reality. In social science, Weber argued, one must avoid confusing comparative results, diagnostic insights and interpretive achievements with the discovery of laws of social development or objectively valid criteria for justifying or criticizing the evaluative ideals that motivate actual conduct.

For this reason, of course, Max Weber's name has become synonymous with one of the central obstacles to solving the intellectual crises and impasses in modern social and political theory.[2] If political philosophers (of all persuasions) have familiarized themselves with any aspect of Weber's work, it has usually been for the purpose of contesting Weber's insistence on the separation between facts and values. Questions about the choiceworthiness of "substantive" value-postulates or evaluative premises, which Weber claims *must* be the focus of practical and political life, are deemed by him not to be resolvable by rational or scientific analysis. This is because science properly deals with considerations about the problem situation in which those postulates may be chosen or accepted, or the problem situation which a given evaluative standpoint may bring about. Consequently, there is no way of moving from a rational understanding of the context that frames our choices or the consequences that might follow from the implementation of a given choice to a rational judgement about which substantive

---

[1] Donald N. Levine, *The Flight from Ambiguity*, chs. 7 and 9.

[2] See also Stephen Turner and Regis Factor, *Max Weber and the Dispute over Reason and Value*.

postulate is worth choosing.[3]   Some have concluded that, for Weber, any value-judgement is itself simply an expression of an arbitrary subjective preference for a given or proposed state of affairs. Although it is debatable whether this picture of Weber as a nihilistic or emotivist thinker is accurate,[4] one line of discussion in this study deals with the consequences of moral skepticism in the context of philosophical debates rather than from the standpoint of Weber's social theory of modernity. To be sure, any attempt to defend liberal values must itself contend with the view of moral-evaluative issues which reduces them to choices among competing "faiths" (liberalism being one of them) whose conflict cannot be rationally settled. In chapter five below I examine Leo Strauss' argument that Weber, as a moralist, knew he had entered a realm in which liberalism, and its attendent value of "intellectual integrity," had to sanction either intolerance to faith or an unqualified commitment to private dogmatism over reason.

Strauss believes that Weber knew he was on the precipice of nihilism. For his part, Weber proposed that all human attachments to ideas and interests can, in a certain respect, be clarified by reason. He also believed that although social theorists must have an abiding interest in informing the possible evaluative stances of his or her own world, this does not lead to contradiction with the aim of value-neutrality or objectivity. On the other hand he knew he could neither eliminate nor rationally control the inevitable element of subjectivity in knowledge. Nevertheless Weber claimed not to embrace wholeheartedly an irrationalist or nihilist interpretation of his doctrine of the infinite "complexity" of (historical) reality.

Max Scheler was perhaps the first thinker to argue that Weber wrongly supposed he could prevent a lapse into nihilism by the sheer power of nominalist thinking. According to Scheler Weber's doctrine of ideal types is the attempt to substitute a capricious constructivism for genuine philosophy:

---

[3] See Weber, "The meaning of 'Ethical Neutrality' in Sociology and Economics," in *The Methodology of the Social Sciences*.

[4] This point is made in a parallel way in Richard Bernstein, *The Restructuring of Social and Political Theory*, pp. 45–50.

[the] power [of Weber's ideal typical concepts] to order the given facts of experience has to be proved in practice, and justified in terms of its opportunistic usefulness. They are not even meant to represent value types or ideal types in the sense of ideal value, but only average types in the sense of self-made models. Admittedly, Max Weber does not reveal the secret of how the formation of such concepts is possible without being led by the spirit to a genuine grasp of *ideas*, nor how one could even find the directions in which it would be possible and permissible to typify and idealize, nor did he observe that *value* decisions are implicit in the *choice* of typical-concepts favoured by himself (for example) even where their content seems to lack any emphasis on value.[5]

Whatever its merits, Scheler's insight here ignores the fact that Weber was intensely aware of the directing role of value interests in defining the problems of science, especially the social sciences, since this is implied by his doctrine of "value relevance."

Karl Jaspers, for example, regarded the problem of value relevance as the challenge at the center of Weber's work. In his view, value relevance designates the possibility of responsible knowledge in a disenchanted age, that is, in an age in which human beings must draw their values from their deepest selves. It is an attempt to establish the possibility of knowledge that could aspire to be both objective and critical while acknowledging that human meanings, human truths, ultimately rest only on contingency.

As we shall see, the claim that rational understandings of meaning can be built upon an awareness of the irreducibly selective activity of the inquirer are subject to considerable doubt. Weber's critics, from Scheler to Strauss 30 years later, maintain that with this idea he celebrates the irrationality at the heart of human life. In other words behind his 'nominalism' is the least innocent kind of 'essentialism'. The troubling implication of his thought, therefore, is a declaration of the failure of philosophy itself, since he places theoretical reflection in the service of absolutized inner (demonic) demands of subjectivity that can never be rationally criticized.

---

[5] Max Scheler, "Max Weber's Exclusion of Philosophy (On the Psychology and Sociology of Nominalist Thought)," in P. Lassman and I. Velody, *Max Weber's Science as a Vocation*, p. 97.

Yet according to Jaspers and later thinkers like Karl Löwith, Weber's strength resided in his ability to dramatize the aporias of modern reason. Some of these can be summarized in the following statements:

1. Science can supply decision makers with technically useful information but it cannot lesson the demand to decide among conflicting values in the dilemmas and struggles of practical life.

2. Objective knowledge can improve our understanding of the relative consequences of adherence to a value system, but it cannot tell us which value system is most choiceworthy.

3. The qualities of a scientific specialist are distinct from those of someone who is sensitive to the culturally empowering or dis-empowering developments in one's society.

4. The commitment to formal rationality in political and socio-economic life often conflicts with the goal of substantive rationality.

As Löwith put it, Weber does not so much aim at resolving contradictions as at a "definitive affirmation of the productivity of contradiction."[6] Or, as Jaspers put it, only historically committed thought, thought that stems from fragmentation and is doomed to partiality, can individualize and particularize one's context sufficiently to permit thought to gain its uncompromising reach for clarity. In a world that has become disenchanted by science, and in which the insolubility of value conflicts has come to appear inevitable, the human relevance of science can be preserved only by seeing reality as an "infinite problem."[7]

In this sense Weber's famous dichotomy between facts and values would not be a distortion of reality but the mark of a discipline necessary for intellectual integrity because it reminds the scientist that his or her work is transcended by unavoidable cultural diversity and conflict and that even a value-free social science would have to include the aim of preserving the dignity of "science-free values."[8] Hence, one

---

[6] Löwith, *Max Weber and Karl Marx*, p. 59.

[7] Karl Jaspers, *On Max Weber*, p. 95.

[8] We will explore this point again in later chapters. See also Leo Strauss, *Natural Right and History*, p. 42.

might claim, with Jaspers, that the fact/value distinction does not lead to intellectual stalemate precisely because it is not Weber's last word. In fact Weber wants to avoid sheer surrender to the aporias of reason, whereby, according to Jaspers, one would be led to avoid responsibility for one's judgements. But for this one must realize that value freedom itself is only a partial beginning, in science, for the search for responsibility or intellectual integrity *toward* the sphere of values.[9] It was only by the sheer force of his genius and personal virtuosity, that Weber could maintain his refusal to "forget about objectivity while valuing, or the possible valuations in the case of objective discussions."[10] On the one hand, Jaspers remarks, this difficult balancing act explains why Weber's work seems ill-suited to fostering followers. For Jaspers, Weber did not pursue scientific objectivity on the grounds that it would be an instrument of human improvement, as in the liberal view. Rather Weberian "objectivity" is an ambiguous stance, one that uneasily combines a distance from conventionally accepted evaluations (including those regarding science) with a direct concern for one's present.

Some thinkers have seen the need to approach Weber more selectively, reconstructing his thought so as to accentuate those aspects that might enrich liberal social theory. Raymond Aron, for example, has argued that Weber's nihilism, his preference for a tragic view of reality, is unwarranted, and even confused, as Strauss perceives. But Aron claims that this should not cause us to obscure the merits of Weber's general view of culture and value pluralism. Against Strauss Aron claims that it was not nihilistic to describe modern belief systems as competing "impersonal forces" as Weber did in "Science as a Vocation." Rather it is only misleading to view values simply as arbitrary systems of preferences. The important focus in Weber's work is the question of how, and with what effect on their capacity for action and thought, human beings formulate, and become subject to, the *requirements* of values. Weber's thought is inconsistent, therefore, only

---

[9] Jaspers, *On Max Weber*, pp. 90–1.

[10] Ibid., p. 11; The image of intellectual integrity that Löwith distils from Weber is that of a kind of heroism which seeks to heighten one's own self-affirmation without lapsing into self-conceit. (*Max Weber and Karl Marx*, pp. 59–60.)

if it is taken as a recommendation that one should be indifferent to the question of how the validity of values is itself established.[11]

To this extent the political and socio-historical fact of value pluralism does not by itself invalidate the search for true meaning or genuine justice as Weber apparently suggests.

> The expression *war of the gods* is the result of translating an indisputable fact (individuals have conjured up incompatible representations of the world) into a philosophy that no one lives by nor subscribes to, because it is contradictory (all representations are equivalent, none being either true or false).[12]

According to Aron, Weber's historical sociology is most fruitful when it shows how socially effective truth claims are in need of relentless clarification. Even Weber suggests that science makes sense not only as a way of pointing to the disparate, inconclusive and problematic way in which meaning is experienced, but also as a way of stimulating new attempts to find solutions to the goal of clarifying meaning. Science can preserve its integrity, confine itself to the goal of providing clarity, only by showing that such solutions depend upon extra-scientific decisions and events. In this respect Weber's deliberately artificial view of human truths—embodied in his ideal-typical investigation of meaning—is intended to stimulate an awareness of the contingency of cultural directions and alternatives. This awareness, far from undermining liberal-enlightenment culture actually gives a new depth to the aspirations of human beings to choose freely, and gain self-conscious control of the forces which determine their lives. Weber's thought is therefore convergent with a moral affirmation of liberalism, much like some critical rationalists have claimed. Hence, as we shall see when discussing Weber's affinities with critical rationalism, it can be argued that Weber's own concern with value conflict does not warrant the

---

[11] Raymond Aron, "Max Weber and Modern Social Science," in *History, Truth and Liberty*, p. 352ff; See also, Mark Warren "Max Weber's Liberalism for a Nietzschean World," p. 38.

[12] Aron, "Max Weber and Modern Social Science," p. 371.

conclusion that "thought should yield to, or be dependent on, decisions that are essentially irrational—or that existence can be fully realized in the kind of liberty that would refuse to yield, even to truth."[13]

REASON, FREEDOM AND POLITICS

Although Weber states that value judgements cannot be rational in an objective sense, he does suggest that they can and must be an essential component of one's stance as a subjectively free actor.[14] As commentators from Karl Löwith to Levine have pointed out, Weber's conception of subjective freedom requires rationality, either in the sense of self-conscious commitment to ends or, in the sense of a capacity to adjust our actions on the basis of insight into constraints, consequences and the costs of alternative courses of action. But this leads to a problem for interpreting the overall meaning and direction of Weber's work. On the one hand Weber seems to say that the capacity for rational action is the condition of freedom, while in another sense—articulated in some famous sections of his substantive sociology—contemporary social embodiments of rationalization have taken the form of an 'iron cage' which may pose a threat to freedom.

In this sense a better understanding of Weber's notion of freedom is called for, and can perhaps be gained by comparing his thought to the tradition of Rousseau and Kant. Like many of the political philosophers and social theorists writing in the aftermath of this tradition, Weber is both a theorist of alienation *and* of positive freedom. To be free, in Weber's sense, is to live in a rationally conscious way without internally or externally sacrificing that autonomy to one's socially contingent situation. But Weber treats the moral foundation of liberal democratic freedoms not as an independent basis for political legitimacy, but at best as a developmental ingredient of modernization. For Weber it makes no

---

[13] Ibid., p. 373.

[14] Habermas therefore distinguishes Weber's ethical scepticism from emotivism: "The former leaves untouched the existential nature of value bonds, whereas the latter explains moral intuitions away by reducing them to emotional dispositions and attitudes." (Habermas, *Moral Consciousness and Communicative Action*, p. 187); See chapter 2 below for MacIntyre's assertion that Weber's work is the key to understanding modernity as an emotivist culture.

sense to think of a liberal democratic society, or any other society, as a moral order in the Kantian-Rousseauian sense, as an order which is founded on the recognition of the dignity of basic rights or rational capacities shared by everyone. This is largely because, for Weber, modernity involves the conscious differentiation of politics and morality, so that politics is always in competition with the aims of moral solidarity. He even suggests that the intrinsic relation of politics to coercive action will always prove a more consistent basis for rationalization than a recognition of the aims of moral solidarity. The modern state is defined by the monopoly of the legitimate means of coercion. This permits the sphere of legal political control to develop as an impersonal order of "rational regulations" providing a calculable, predictable environment ultimately adapted to a greater range of organized interests in the society.

Weber acknowledges that, despite the fact that the modern state is institutionally organized for strategic actions and decisions, it has been dignified by appeal to its rationally justifiable and universalistic standards. Likewise, from the standpoint of the aims of morality the focus of these institutions must be seen as an unprincipled concession to the needs of power.[15] For Weber, a legitimate order can be sociologically intelligible only on the basis of the probable effects of empirical beliefs—however they are cultivated, and whatever ends are thereby made possible—rather than on the basis of the rational justifiability of its moral principles. Therefore the legitimation claims of the modern state can be based only nominally on the criterion of popular control or free consent. There is no way of sociologically defining modern legitimacy on the basis of the idea that members of society would in reality, or virtually, be subject only to laws of their own making.

Rousseau knew that any version of liberal democracy, conceived as an ideally rational social order, required a realistic sociological conception of solidality and democratic autonomy. This was expressed in his view that individuals had to be forced to be free. Weber, on the other hand, proposes that the realistic aspect of liberal democratic politics consists in a kind of adaptation to a particular kind of rationality

---

[15] Weber, *Economy and Society*, vol. 1, p. 600.

available only to interests that orient themselves to the competition for strategic advantages. To be rational in politics is to take account of the fact that there can be no substantively rational way of deciding among social choices. It is notable that Weber refrained from a conservative, romantic, or politically spurious aristocratic-individualist, reaction to the tradition of the liberal democratic Enlightenment. Rather he adopted a kind of negative, or pragmatic, allegiance to liberal democratic values expressed in his statement that "it is a gross self-deception to believe that without the achievements of the age of the Rights of Man any one of us, including the most conservative, can go on living his life."[16] Nevertheless, Weber's political sociology portrays the modern secular order as a question mark for liberal democrats. He never disputes the notion that modern institutions ought to make it possible for individuals to formulate personally consistent commitments and choices, and to determine rationally the effective means for carrying out those choices. But the goals associated with the various embodiments of this ideal—such as individualist freedoms, the enhancement of a politically mature national culture or social equality—have become undermined and consumed by the very means set up to serve them.

This is largely the result of the development of bureaucracy according to Weber. However, against the temptation to regard his analysis as a precursor to Daniel Bell's "end of ideology" thesis, it must be remembered that bureaucratization is never considered politically neutral in Weber's work. To be sure, bureaucracy has formalized the criteria of access and terms of membership around which the dominant spheres of society are organized, guaranteeing impersonal and officially non-arbitrary treatment of the abilities and "life-chances" of the individuals placed under them. But the ideals motivating the development of modern rationalization are less relevant to defining the political reality of modern society than the kinds of attitudes, personalities and institutional formulas of power and discipline that are typically and selectively developed under those conditions. Bureaucratic capitalism may signal a kind of "end of ideology," but as a mode of authority or domination it does not have an ethically, or politically, neutral signifi-

---

[16] Weber, "Parliament and Government in a Reconstructed Germany," Appendix II, *Economy and Society*, vol. 2, p. 1403.

cance. In fact Weber insists that, even by regulating competition and pacifying social conflict, no set of institutions that can eliminate the form of struggle which takes place as "selection." Rather one can only shift the means by which struggle (and therefore, selection) is carried on, changing the consequences it has for those whose lives are at stake in it or for the human qualities that are privileged or disadvantaged by it.[17]

In what sense, then, is Weber a theorist of human freedom? For Weber freedom is not *positively* achieved by guaranteeing certain rights, opportunities or by recognizing principles of human dignity. Rather freedom becomes ethically meaningful for him as a self-formative quality of persons or "personalities" that can and must prove itself in the realistic conditions of action. As we shall see, Weber also regarded modernity (to the diminishing extent that it remains tied to a specific outcome of religious rationalization) as a cultural experiment for making autonomy and freedom a challenge for the inner life of the individual. Thus, for Weber, a genuine "personality" is one whose life is intrinsically related to values and meanings worth struggling for,[18] one whose commitment to goals is not determined by habit and socially contingent interests.

If one takes account of some of his rather *ad hoc* elaborations of this idea Weber may appear to be in the thrall of a Romantic, Nietzschean conception of individuality through which he views the problems of politics and social distinction. Wilhelm Hennis, for example, presents an account of Weber's unqualified indebtedness to Nietzsche's thought. Weber's central concern, according to Hennis, was with the character-forming importance of personalistic ethical heroism which has been depreciated by the elimination of creative ethical struggle in modern culture and the eudaemonistic orientation of modern liberalism.[19] Hennis reminds us of Weber's often ignored remark that social science

---

[17] For Weber's important concept of "selection" in society see *Economy and Society*, vol. 1, pp. 55-6, and "The Meaning of 'Ethical Neutrality'", p. 27.

[18] Weber, *Roscher and Knies: The Logical Problems of Historical Economics*, p. 192; Weber, "Objectivity in Social Science and Social Policy," in *Methodology of the Social Sciences*, p. 57.

[19] Hennis, *Max Weber: Essays in Reconstruction*, ch. 5.

is evaluative in so far as it poses the question of how ill-adapted or well-adapted a society is to the rise of certain determinate "human types": "[Weber's] work no longer appears to be a 'sociology', that is, a science that, if anything, seeks to establish the quality of a social order; [rather] the quality of the society is then only a *means* for the real question concerning the *Typus Mensch* promoted or suppressed by these means."[20]

Some, however, have contested the nostalgia underpinning Weber's conviction that a 'genuine personality' may now be less likely to flourish in those societies that have undergone modernization.[21] The embodiment of inner freedom, or subjective freedom, in a "personality" appears to be more essential to Weber's anthropological depiction of human needs and capacities than the embodiment of autonomy through intersubjectively constituted action and reform. Weber seems to be saying that rationalization and the break with traditional authority have made possible the achievement of both individuation and democratization but that now individuality has been cheapened and politics has been engulfed by the rival claims of moralists and bureaucrats. Our paradoxical world of both "sterile excitation" and the bureaucratic iron cage has become stripped of meaning for those who would become "personalities." Bryan Turner has argued that in this respect Weber's work is informed primarily by the "tragic history" of personality. According to Turner, Weber privileges rationality seen as "an heroic act

---

[20] Ibid., p. 152.

[21] For instance Colin Gordon has remarked that one must qualify any globally pessimistic reading of Weber's disenchantment [*Entzauberung*] thesis: "There seems to be little basis for attributing to Weber the belief that the disenchantment of the world was a threshold of mutation that could be negotiated only at the price of unbearable moral sacrifices. What he appears to have wanted to convey was rather that different societies arrive at that threshold—for reasons that his sociology undertakes to elucidate—endowed with very variable levels of capability for negotiating it successfully...The edge of Weber's criticism is turned not so much against the process of *Entzauberung* as such, as against the spurious and immature compensations for *Entzauberung* resorted to by his fellow Germans: the mass reproduction of the 'parvenu aristocratic' Junker personality, the eclectic epidemic of private quests for *Erlebnis*." (Gordon, "The Soul of the Citizen: Max Weber and Michel Foucault on Rationality and Government," in S. Whimster and S. Lash, eds., *Max Weber, Rationality and Modernity*, pp. 312–11).

worked out against the mundane world" while depreciating "rational adaptation to the contingency of ordinary life."[22] Like Talcott Parsons, he believes Weber was too hasty in describing the revolution in "external" freedom and institutional rationality afforded by the formally rational institutions of modern society as an initial cultural breakthrough that has worn thin under the weight of organizational imperatives which have become merely technically indispensable for systems of domination.[23]

BUREAUCRACY AND THE EXPROPRIATION OF POLITICS

There can be no doubt that, in terms of Weber's political sociology, bureaucracy exemplifies the paradoxical consequences of rationalization and modern democratic freedom. As a "legitimate order," bureaucracy is based on a "belief in legality." This belief is a kind of confidence in the fact that authority and binding decisions are the result of formally correct enactments. Democracy itself requires that responsibility for, and criteria of, decision making have been objectively determined, and that arbitrariness gives way to competence, due process and rules that follow rationally from general norms.[24] Bureaucracy, however, is also a form of "domination" which can be considered the "typical expression" of the formal type of authority Weber calls "legal-rational."[25] Hence, while its authority is based on impersonal rules and objectively certifiable competence, as a form of domination bureaucracy rests on the ability to enforce adaptation to technical-organizational imperatives. While Marx proposed that the expropriative domination of capital over labour is achieved and expressed in the separation of the worker from the means of production, Weber argued that the separation of the official from the means of administration expressed nothing more than a technically irresistible trend. This leads to a situation whereby members of organizations are subject to a uniquely meaningless expropriation of

---

[22] Bryan S. Turner, *Citizenship and Capitalism: The Debate over Reformism*, p. 125.
[23] See, for example, Weber, *Economy and Society*, vol. 2, p. 1399ff; On the ambiguously revolutionary character of bureaucracy see Ibid., p. 1116.
[24] Ibid., p. 991.
[25] Ibid., p. 992.

responsibility. At the same time, the ritualized adherence to routine and impersonal rules often serves no other purpose than to normalize the privileges of office and expertise.[26] Experts will often seek to monopolize the definition of problems, circumventing new or alternative definitions, so as to make their expertise seem unassailable. Of course, Weber observes that bureaucracy requires an informal concentration of politics, or goal-setting authority, at the top of the organization. But it is there that the stifling contest between experts and dilettantes normally takes over.[27]

Weber characterized bureaucracy as a socially revolutionary force, but one which cannot achieve its specific function of efficiency in the service of pre-given goals except at the risk of rigid control and the "stereotyping of action." This is no doubt why the type of authority which he contrasted with bureaucracy and its functionalization of authority is that of charismatic authority. Charisma is the capacity to motivate and organize the actions of human beings purely by the force of evocation. It is characterized as a break with routine. Its underlying capacity to define matters of moral seriousness in a culture cannot be judged in terms of accountability to utilitarian or rational considerations about the ends or means of action.[28] It is not surprising then that so many commentators have traced this concept back to Nietzsche (albeit in a way that Weber never acknowledged). Weber's important concept of the "routinization of charisma" basically coincides with Nietzsche's recognition of the way in which the achievements of great individuals can ultimately become socially effective and understandable only when

---

[26] *Economy and Society,* vol. 1, p. 290.

[27] *Economy and Society*, vol. 2, p. 1417; See also H.T. Wilson, *The American Ideology*, p. 206, where the democratic possibilities of this informal refuge of politics atop bureaucracy are characterized as follows: "The progress of bureaucratization in public administration occurs parallel to the emergence of mass democracy as a political threat to disorder. Meritocracy and mass democracy go hand in hand, the first a perversion of equality directed to the permanent expansion of 'free labour,' the second a distortion of equality which defines it in terms of the right to spectate and consume. The governors, though they may attempt to resist the social levelling bureaucracy favours, are ultimately consumed by it themselves."

[28] *Economy and Society*, vol. 2, p. 1111ff.

they are made functional for their society, or when their "mission" is codified so as to adapt it to the demands of routine, institutionalized action.[29]

There is one sense in which Weber, as opposed to Nietzsche, believed that charismatic forces could effectively assert themselves against the forces of spiritual petrification in modern society. Weber intimated that liberal democracy could avoid being hijacked by bureaucracy only if was turned into a means for recruiting charismatic leaders through plebiscitary competition.[30] The object of democratic politics would no longer be more than a formal, fictional accountability to the will of the people. Weber stands as one of great theorists of competitive-elite democracy who argued that the paradoxes of democratic party politics, with its mobilization of mass opinion, could only be overcome indirectly—that is, through a process of recruitment through acclamation.[31] He wanted to show how democracy could be converted into a means for steering the forces of political "selection" so that leadership and personality might converge at the top. Turner and Factor summarize his thinking precisely:

> The plebiscitarian form that he promoted as a constitutional structure served to *make* values compete by subjecting their charismatic champions to the test of public acclamation. In this ideal we see the last vestige of the liberal faith in public discussion—no longer as a faith in its rationality, but as a faith in the power of leadership appeals to command voluntary devotion.[32]

In this connection Weber shared with Nietzsche the idea that democratic politics could only provide a backdrop for testing value-standpoints in terms of the intrinsically rare human qualities that could bear them most authentically. Despite his qualified acceptance of liberal democratic institutions, Weber believed that the challenges of politics could not be

---

[29] Ibid., p. 1135; Cf. Friedrich Nietzsche, *The Will to Power*, nos. 876–886.

[30] This idea is developed in *Economy and Society*, vol. 2, pp. 1393ff.

[31] On these connections see David Beetham, *Max Weber and the Theory of Modern Politics*.

[32] Stephen Turner and Regis Factor, "Decisionism and Politics: Weber as Constitutional Theorist," in Whimster and Lash, eds., *Max Weber, Rationality and Modernity*, p. 352.

understood in democratic terms. On the virtues of democracy he was moved to say: "Perhaps the necessity of maintaining one's inner dignity in the midst of a democratic world can serve as a test of the genuineness of dignity."[33]

Weber's analysis of bureaucracy (and the politics of mass opinion) presents serious obstacles to any political theory that would anticipate social embodiments of freedom and rationality capable of overcoming social relations based on power and ideology. Herbert Marcuse saw in Weber's work a stultifying, but unacknowledged, identification of technology and domination. However, it is hard to agree with Marcuse that Weber was "indifferent" to the question of the "substantive" content of technical reason—that is, its projection of "what a society intends to do with men and things."[34] Indeed Weber saw the institutionalization of non-coercive, non-ascriptive relations among formally free subjects in the areas of law, administration and the market as only one side of the destiny of modern humanity. In a democratic context, bureaucracy is devised for the sake of creating rational, post-traditional, non-coercive relations, adapted to a world in which rationally depersonalized rules regulate access to wealth, power and status within functionally specific domains. But the rational, formally non-coercive character of bureaucratic domination is, in substantive terms, something quite different. Bureaucracy has become a refinement of the means for exercising power and domination rather than an institutionalization of liberal democratic normative standards in regulating the struggle for wealth, power and status. As Michael Foucault might have said, the formal rationality and non-coerciveness normally intended by both bureaucracy and the marketplace is entirely consistent with the substantively irrational and coercive, or disciplinary, exercise of power. What Marcuse objected to in Weber was the failure to offer a new, non-bureaucratic path toward substantive rationality as the ultimate goal of political practice. The inherent tendency toward substantive irrationality and complacent opportunism in bureaucracy, appears to Weber as the

---

[33] Weber, "National Character and the Junkers," in *From Max Weber: Essays in Sociology*, p. 393.

[34] Herbert Marcuse, "Industrialism and Capitalism in the Thought of Max Weber," in *Negations*, p. 224.

modern form of meaninglessness. No exact equivalent appears in Marxism which tries to locate new sources of practical-political meaning in the conditions for overcoming historically contingent substantive irrationality and systematically concealed coercion.[35] As Habermas has argued, Weber never tried to close the gap between the promise of modern ideals and their selective implementation. Nor can Weber's view be assimilated to that of the liberal sociology of Talcott Parsons who celebrated the plurality of spheres of meaning (and certain trends toward non-bureaucratic authority) as a boon for liberal individualism. As we shall see in the next chapter, Weber held the view that the non-coercive force of authority and administered culture provide perhaps a more effective basis for "domination" than does direct coercion or economic power. In this regard echoes of Weber's thought are to be found in later critical theorists such as the thinkers of the Frankfurt School and Foucault.

Hence, if Weber is a theorist of "alienation", he is one who is not easy to assimilate into those trends in political philosophy or social theory which try to provide an ameliorative reconstruction of the modern project. His "other side" of modernity involves a process whereby the techniques, social institutions and systems of authority in the name of which people have sought freedom, meaning and a rationally expedient order have actually come to rule over them. In his critique of socialism, Weber actually pays homage to Marx's analysis of the tendency of the means to dominate over the end.[36] Indeed the paradox of unintended consequences is a central element of Weber's thought,[37] and it seems to apply most glaringly to the purposes of Marxism and liberal Enlightenment culture. Although a line of social theorists from Rousseau to Durkheim and Parsons envisage a society in which the reconciliation between authority and human dignity, or between "obedience and liberty,"[38] would be ideally possible, Weber

---

[35] B. Turner, *Capitalism and Citizenship*, p. 141.

[36] Weber, "Socialism," in *Max Weber: The Interpretation of Social Reality*, p. 202.

[37] The best account of Weber's own views on this subject and the literature surrounding it may be found in J.G. Merquior, *Rousseau and Weber: Two Studies in the Theory of Legitimacy,* pp. 165–68, 180.

[38] Jean-Jacques Rousseau, *The Social Contract*, bk. III, ch. XII.

leaves us with observations about the paradoxes of the institutions founded in the name of modern freedoms and, more generally, an "antinomical"[39] approach to the very questions themselves.

IS LIBERAL DEMOCRATIC
THOUGHT COHERENT?

Weber's view of positive freedom emphasizes the development of autonomous personhood and its importance to those modern virtues, such as a sense of "vocation", he obviously commends and wants to promote. But Weber's adherence to a conception of positive freedom is set against the background of his account of the threat to individuality presented by the practices and institutions dominating the modern social order. In chapter two we examine how this tension and incommensurability is not just observed by Weber, but, in a certain sense, is actually built into his basic theory of social action and social relationships. But in subsequent chapters we look at this issue in the context of contemporary critiques and reconstructions of liberal democratic theory and its intellectual foundations. In what follows it will therefore be necessary to discuss some traditional and recent controversies about the status of liberal democracy as an intellectual tradition and a philosophical system.

Some political theorists have recently argued that Weber fails to see how the goods of autonomous selfhood and character that he emphasized as a theorist of positive freedom could be realized only by a more genuine democratic community than the kind he was prepared to contemplate.[40] These writers would like to restore to liberal theory those substantive elements of "the ethical life" (*Sittlichkeit,* in Hegel's terminology) that caused thinkers like Rousseau and Hegel to return to

---

[39] This is the apt phrase used by Mommsen to characterize Weber's manner of thinking through the problematic substance of modern social and political life. Wolfgang Mommsen, "The Antinomical Structure of Max Weber's Political Thought," in *The Political and Social Theory of Max Weber*, pp 24–43.

[40] A good example is Alan Gilbert, *Democratic Individuality*. Gilbert, aside from comparing Weber's approach to his own amalgam of Marx and Aristotle, makes the following point (p. 348) about Weber's reduction of democracy to leadership competition: "On that empiricist view, the meaning of a term is reduced to whatever measures it; we cannot have a (radical) democratic theory but only a description of 'current' democratic practices."

Aristotle. To the extent that they do return to Aristotle they partially echo his attempt to relate the moral problems of human existence to the essential character of politics as a human telos.

Liberalism's pre-social conception of selfhood and its abstract account of justice as the result of rationally motivated cooperation has been duly criticized by thinkers such as Rousseau, Hegel, Mill, Marx, Dewey, Critical theorists and communitarians. In chapter three I examine Alasdaire MacIntyre's attempt to attribute the dilemmas of liberalism to the faulty premises of modern moral discourse. In a nutshell, MacIntyre argues that a society is bound to produce an incoherent moral theory, and intractable political controversies, if it tailors its morality to considerations about what human beings can be when they are uniting for the purposes of protecting their rights, or maximizing their utility, as opposed to what they can be when their moral concepts deal with the kinds of ends or purposes that should inform their striving. MacIntyre argues, like other communitarians such as Roberto Unger and Michael Sandel, that liberalism goes wrong when it becomes a morality of rules and abstract principles rather than a morality of purposes.[41] However, according to MacIntyre, one can also turn to Weber's description of the modern world to understand the failures of liberalism. In particular he notes that the rational and universalistic moral epistemology of liberal doctrine actually undermines itself when translated into the actual practices and forms of human agency which Weber viewed as prevalent in modern societies. According to MacIntyre, our "Weberian" world exhibits polarized spheres of social meaning, and separates the phenomena related to individuality and arbitrary personal freedom on the one hand from those of organization or impersonal domination on the other. The gap between these two spheres can be bridged, and modernity itself justified, only by disguising successful power as efficiency and subjectivism as autonomy. We will see how MacIntyre portrays Weber's stifling dualisms as a symptom of the congenital inability of the modern moral tradition to provide a viable conception of the "virtues".

Other theorists addressed in this study, such as Habermas and

---

[41] See Roberto Unger, *Knowledge and Politics*, chs. 2 and 3; Michael Sandel, *Liberalism and the Limits of Justice*.

Rorty, must be seen as the successors of those modern political philosophers who have at least partially identified liberal democracy with the worthy achievements of modernity. They join earlier figures like Rousseau and Hegel in attributing the discontents of modernity to forces within thought and social reality that have caused liberalism to misfire as a theory of society and a mode of socialization.

For Rousseau the solution to the internal dilemmas of liberal democratic thought, specifically the tension between the universal and the particular, depended upon a diagnosis of the history of the movement from nature to society. His approach, of course, was developed in terms of the Enlightenment goal of perfecting human relationships by reason. But Rousseau also complicated Enlightenment thought by asserting an ineluctable tension between, on the one hand, the adaptation of human lives to the contingent and conventional requirements of communities and, on the other hand, normative ideals whose validity can be established in a self-sufficient manner. This leads to a philosophy that cannot easily meet its own requirement to reconcile authentic selfhood and republican virtue.[42] The relevant point here, however, is that Rousseau tried to recover the resources of classical republicanism and Aristotelian philosophy where politics is defined as a self-sufficient *type* of relationship which completes relationships of differentiation and convenience.[43] But for Aristotle, as opposed to moderns like Rousseau, politics is the sphere in which human beings are directed toward the realization of their essential nature as moral beings. The theory of justice that Rousseau offers is based on an anthropology distinguishing the sphere of morality, where the term "virtue" applies, from the sphere of nature, where only the concept of goodness applies.[44]

Before Rousseau, liberalism had its intellectual roots in Hobbesian moral science which was directly in conflict with Aristotelianism and its assumption that the realm of shared values and constitutive moral identity can provide a foundation of practical reasoning. The compari-

---

[42] Rousseau, "Du bonheur public" (fragment), *Oeuvres completes*, v. III, Paris, 1964, p. 510.

[43] Aristotle, *Politics*, Bk. I, Ch. 2, Bk II, Ch. 2 and Bk. III, Ch. 9.

[44] Rousseau, "A Discourse on the Origin of Inequality," in G.D.H. Cole, ed., *The Social Contract and Discourses*, pp. 60, 71, 91.

son between the two traditions displays their different normative stances toward the problem of rationally relating the interests and qualities of human agents to the social order. The Aristotelian approach asserts that there are natural and potentially corrupt forms of social action and relationships, and that justice in a given political community consists in the former ruling over the latter. This of course requires practical knowledge and prudence since for Aristotle the ideally best form of life can only be applied to a material and social context whose nature cannot be abstractly known. Justice requires the right material, which, for human beings, is never independent of the results of habit or socialization. In morality one is always dealing with the need to balance a model of the good life as a theoretical object with the kinds of human qualities and social-environmental conditions under which the good life can be realized in practice. This is why the realization of moral being is political for Aristotle: determinations about the source of ethical value cannot be referred to a prepolitical standard such as would be implied if the "good" were to be reducible to the "pleasant." Rather such determinations have to be made in light of the kind of person appropriate to certain kinds of relationships and activities, with the result that justice is a kind of 'naturalness', modeled on the attainment of happiness from the internal worth of the activity itself. Politics is therefore a matter of rewarding and cultivating the right kind of people for the relevant activities, and the justice of a state consists in doing this in a way that makes people capable of a pattern of worthy action.

By contrast, standard liberal democracy is based on a philosophical defense of arrangements that would allow a peaceful regulation of affairs among persons in the light of the pre-moral, if not pre-social, understanding of their needs, desires and interests. This leads to a doctrine that either views human nature as politically and socially deficient (as Leo Strauss would say) or which asserts the ultimately subjective nature of value choices. In either case principles of political obligation are derived from the notion of a rational social contract, a model that serves this tradition well. A morality whose principles could be acceptable to any rational individual rests on a theoretical account of the nature of humanity's most basic needs, passions and interests. But it also depends upon the idea that the sphere of individuality could be almost automatically immunized from alienation and arbitrary power. This goal of freedom, as opposed to Aristotelian "happiness" or "virtue," requires only the most undemanding moral premises, namely, that one recognize the self-evident advantages of an agreement to accept mutual restraints which would serve any rational person's self-interest. Political theory is relieved of the demand that the relevant moral force in society would derive from the fact that people do, or ought to, share a life in which only the 'truly happy' fulfill standards of moral achievement. In Aristotle a *polis* is a moral unity precisely because its citizens are related to one another first, as the kind of people to whom its standards of moral achievement can be justified and, secondly, by the possibility of recognizing the distinctiveness of those in whose actions the relevant virtues can be exemplified.

This stands in contrast to the liberalism of John Locke who argued that political justice exists for the sake of the integrity of pre-political social intercourse and which can be guaranteed by institutions that are accountable only for preserving that integrity. Lockean liberalism rejects the view that justice involves the promotion of (and predisposition toward) human qualities and satisfactions that are distinctively political. For Locke, everyone can be sufficiently educated in civic morality by exercizing their own private freedom and responsibility for themselves. In fact liberalism itself is often identified with the idea that truth and justice can prevail in politics only to the degree that people can openly exercize their specifically private freedom.

However, as Rousseau points out, the ideal rationality of social and political arrangements had itself been defined arbitrarily by his predecessors. Their judgements about what would be achieved if social relationships were ordered rationally could not be justified except in a circular way. It was necessary for them to think of the advantages of civic morality as a matter of exchanging the inconvenience of mutual aggressiveness and selfish power in the state of nature for the convenience of institutions that allow peace and civic virtue to triumph in the realm of selfishness.[45] According to Rousseau, by attributing the achievement of civic virtue to institutions that are merely means for

---

[45] Ibid., pp. 47, 71–2.

controlling the effects of unsociability, liberalism had defined freedom by qualities that are adapted to the corruption, distortion and misuse of freedom. In Rousseau's alternative, freedom is still the highest good, but it cannot be disconnected from the development of needs and interests that lead people to autonomously enjoy themselves in their sociability. People must be both the subject and object of the kind of political association that is constitutive of freedom.

Rousseau differed from Aristotle in that he held that there is no model of civic virtue that is based on naturalness. But he also disagreed with his liberal predecessors' idea that the purpose of liberal institutions would extend no further than reforming the external conditions under which people strive to realize their values and goals. He had the idea that civic virtue requires a kind of moral perfection of denatured human striving itself. Since human beings are the types of creatures whose nature is altered or replaced by an essentially coercive process of socialization, freedom is a paradoxical requirement. A morality of freedom must look for standards of political legitimacy in a type of social bond that can exist for any given empirical society only in a virtual way, that is, as a transcendence of the arbitrariness of the socialization process. Rousseau felt he could compensate for the discrepancy between ideal and reality with his conception of "the legislator" whose artfulness and prudence adapts universalistic morality to the contingencies of society. Rousseau knew that the most important dilemma for a *liberal* politics founded on the universal dignity of human beings lay in the fact that society has no natural ability to *condition itself* as an ideal moral unity.

This, more than the earlier liberal problem of "consent" or "contract," is the foundation of Rousseau's thought. For there is nothing in a consensus that allows one to identify it as an expression of the "general will" except for the deployment of social forces which is necessary to make people competent in regards to their moral freedom. Rousseau saw clearly the dilemmas of the liberalism he inherited, namely that freedom would have to be portrayed as a life of comfortable isolation from others or else, left in its natural state, it would lead to the rule of pure arbitrariness. He therefore needed to make the ideal of freedom infinitely applicable to "reality" or the factors of human socialization and solidarity. The common good, in Rousseau's conception, is therefore the virtual object of one's rational, de-particularized will. Although morally demanding, this introduces the politically convenient result that the people can be mistaken about the general will without really being politically incompetent in their role as participants in a self-governing order. Defined in this way, the moral force of the enactment through which the common good is expressed, and through which the people give the law to themselves, must be imbued with self-sufficiency.

Carl Schmitt argued that it is this logic that gives democracy that self-sufficient value which it normally has in modern political discourse.[46] One consequence of this is that it becomes ever more difficult to distinguish between the interests of the state and those of society. Weber, like Schmitt after him, was concerned that prudence, and the substantive decisions necessary to it, had been made subordinate to the achievement of moral or social ideals. Schmitt, for his part, argued that this insight is obscured by our contemporary hybrid called liberal democracy. He puts most of the blame on the "liberal" component which, he argued, detracts from the independent problems of political life by sustaining the fictions of procedural determinations of the will of the people as well as the "rule of law" which automatically guarantee the rational moral effectiveness of the political process. This puts prudence and sovereignty (norm creating authority) in the hands of those who gain power through processes (like party competition and parliamentary discussion) that, ironically, were devised by liberalism to domesticate prudence and guarantee that decisions will conform to norms. Schmitt therefore worried that the existential primacy of decision and prudence in political relationships had naively been made indistinguishable from social and ethical content. He argued that liberal democracy is blind to what ultimately matters in politics, or its natural distinction—the necessary presence of friend-enemy relationships.[47]

Weber does not adopt this rhetoric, even in his writings dealing with national self-assertion. Many of Weber's discussions of liberal democracy deal with issues related to its sociological ambiguity, such as

---

[46] Carl Schmitt, *The Crisis of Parliamentary Democracy*, p. 25ff.
[47] Schmitt, *The Concept of the Political*.

the gap between social and political democracy and the expropriation of political life by government bureaucracies or party organizations. When he extols the virtue of parliamentary democracy he views it as a possible means of selecting leaders who understand struggle as an autonomous part of politics. But even here there is an irreducible ambiguity since there is nothing in the normative content of liberal democracy that can forestall its slide into mere "negative politics," where techniques of purely formal openness and scrutiny are expected to reform the processes of power rather than make them dynamic and effective.[48]

In these and other areas of Weber's work we shall see how he pre-empts the tasks of normative political theory in favor of a diagnosis of modernity that views the possibility of ethical rationalization in politics with skepticism. From the standpoint of normative political theory, liberal democracy has to do with limiting arbitrary political power and making the conduct of public affairs open and accessible in an effective way to free and informed input from citizens and representative groups. Another important strain of liberal democratic normative theory is the emphasis on freedom from both internal and external dependency. Nevertheless, writers from Weber to Michel Foucault have shown how the liberal social order has sanctioned new forms of domination to replace the older kind which had been dissolved by liberalism's separation between the public and private realm as well as by its affirmation of voluntary social attachments and more diverse types of social identity. In the name of freedoms achieved through the rule of law and protections of voluntary association and property, for instance, liberal democratic societies have not become immune to the opening up of new forms of institutional life characterized by bureaucratic regulation, monopolies of knowledge and concentrations of market power.

To some, these developments require a re-statement, or reconstruction, of the goals of liberal democracy; to others they reveal its bankrupt foundations. In this connection, contemporary "communitarians" have suggested that liberalism is to be blamed for the *de facto* moral arbitrariness of modern politics and society. It is interesting that Weber

---

[48] *Economy and Society*, vol. 2, pp. 979–80, 1407ff; On the discrepancy between social and political democratization see W. Mommsen, "Max Weber and Roberto Michels," in Mommsen, ed., *Max Weber and his Contemporaries*, p. 148.

shares the communitarian insistence on the meta-ethical primacy of politics. But communitarians, as the contemporary representatives of Aristotelian thought, argue that political virtue consists in the attunment of citizens to an ordering of goods that will give a coherent purpose to their lives and connections with others. Failure in this latter respect is held to be a symptom of modernity which has had to make virtues out of vices. They observe how justice and political cooperation have become instrumental to the interests of socially irresponsible individuals rather than types of relationships whose practices are informed directly by a determinate view of the nature of the good life. Weber cuts off the return to Aristotelian thought, not because he wants justice to apply to relationships among people who may have irreconcilable views on the nature of the good life, but rather because of his morally ambiguous notion of an "ethics of responsibility." As we shall see, this approach precludes the search for an independent source of ethical meaning in politics, since in politics one is not responsible for the integrity of a certain view of the good life, but for enduring "morally dangerous" ways of dealing with a given social environment and the moral intention to change it. In this respect Weber's understanding of politics is informed by what William Connolly has called a "post-Nietzschean" social ontology where "the fit between human designs and the material drawn into those designs is always partial, incomplete, and likely to contain an element of subjugation and imposition..."[49]

I have mentioned communitarianism here because, taken in the broadest sense, it has been the bearer of a characteristic anxiety regarding the direction of contemporary discussion on the crises of political theory since Weber. Communitarians argue, for example, that liberalism is at least indirectly responsible for the alleged social and theoretical failures and distortions that have given credibility to the positions of Nietzsche, Weber and Foucault. Liberalism not only erodes forms of life in which identity is conditioned by history and tradition, it also dissolves forms of association and relationship in which action that attaches us to distinctive values and ends must be pursued for its own sake. Of course liberals will reply that these risks of dissolution are the

---

[49] William Connolly, *Identity / Difference*, p. 91.

price to be paid for the considerable moral achievement of separating the sphere of individuality from the systems of generalized rules governing many of the social functions or roles in a modern society. Here, again, the greatest challenge to liberals comes from those like Weber and Foucault who argue that liberal moral goals, like freedom from dependency, introduce new, more discrete or anonymous forms of power. Recognition of rights and societal rationalization may indeed correspond to a process in which individuals remain structurally powerless in some sense, or even become agents in their own subjection. This kind of argument rests on the "post-Nietzschean" thesis that the moral goals of any society inevitably function to uphold social forces and beliefs which are themselves manipulable factors in systems of power and domination.

Paradoxically, something like a communitarian response is necessary to maintain a defense of liberalism in the face of this argument. We will see how Richard Rorty partially incorporates communitarianism into his attempt to defend liberalism as a coherent moral tradition, one in which the meaning and value assigned to its particular moral purposes are not arbitrary. Rorty will argue that "our" liberal community is one in which the contingent meaning and value of its moral purposes is openly recognized, and that one of the key virtues of liberal public openness is not that it might guarantee truth or justice but that it would encourage us not to look for certainties in these matters. In the words of Michael Walzer, both liberals and communitarians could be made to appreciate liberalism as "a morally and politically necessary adaptation to the complexities of modern life."[50] By this he means that liberal democratic societies render communities fragile in order to discover or create environments for appreciating the value of more and different kinds of social ties and identities. In no way does liberalism, as a form of life or as a theory, imply that individuals can somehow transcend the contingencies of their social identities.

Two of the theorists examined in this study, MacIntyre and Habermas, respond to these dilemmas of liberalism by contesting the individualistic premises of modern moral discourse. This is noteworthy

---

[50] Michael Walzer, "Liberalism and the Art of Separation," p. 319.

because MacIntyre is a representative of the communitarian critique while Habermas seeks to rehabilitate the virtues and possibilities of political liberalism for social democracy. Each claims that the latent or overt subjectivism of modern thought leads to the unwarranted assumption that moral perspectives themselves can only be defended as useful beliefs. This leads to the idea that the real, though unacknowledged, weakness of modern discourse is that it cannot answer the question of why one ought to take morality seriously. If, as MacIntyre contends, Nietzsche and Weber simply adopt strategies by which one can avoid this problem altogether, they also share the shortcomings of the modern tradition they want to overcome. It is therefore a short step from the premises of liberal individualism to a perspective that would altogether dismiss the relevance of rationality and truth in moral matters.

Habermas believes that the critical power of the modern ideal of rational consent can be reconstructed in a way that is self-sufficiently moral. Because the activities and relationships of modern society involve the use of "external goods" like money and power, modern social and political systems have been shaped by the imperative to rationalize strategic action. Habermas' work is valuable, as is MacIntyre's, for showing how the dominant pattern of societal modernization has made it difficult to arrive at criteria of political justice that function independently of strategic manipulation. But we will have occasion to question whether MacIntyre can substitute a lament about modernity for a philosophical argument about its moral premises. In a different way we will raise doubts about the relevance of Habermas' attempt to devise an ideal standpoint for moral reasoning whose capacity to resolve actual moral controversies is grounded in an abstraction from the contingent purposes of political or social life.

Finally, we can note that Weber himself shares some important insights with contemporary critics of liberalism, especially regarding liberalism's deep separation of selfhood from politics. In this regard we can recall the words of Michael Sandel, a leading communitarian thinker:

> Liberalism teaches respect for the distance between self and ends, and when this distance is lost, we are submerged in a circumstance that ceases to be ours. But by seeking to secure this distance too completely, liberalism

undermines its own insight. By putting the self beyond the reach of politics, it makes human agency an article of faith rather than an object of continuing attention and concern, a premise of politics rather than its precarious achievement. This misses the pathos of politics and also its most inspiring possibilities. It overlooks the danger that when politics goes badly, not only disappointments but also dislocations are likely to result. And it forgets the possibility that when politics goes well, we can know a good in common that we cannot know alone.[51]

In the next chapter we will see that Weber would have agreed with Sandel's exhortations about the existential significance of politics, but would have found little or no relevance in the call to place politics in the service of a communitarian solution. At the same time much of Weber's social theory undermines the normative justification of the liberal social order. This study addresses the kinds of alternatives available to Weber's perspective. In particular I will consider not only how liberal democracy, and the model of social and political rationality it entails, might be reconstructed to respond to Weber's ambiguous challenge, but also whether, on the contrary, Weber's thought merely exemplifies the distortion of moral-political problems that has marked liberal modernity itself.

---

[51] Sandel, *Liberalism and the Limits of Justice*, p 183.

Chapter Two

THE NECESSITY OF CHOICE:
TOWARD A CONVERGENCE OF
PERSONALITY AND POLITICS

One of Weber's most 'liberal'-sounding themes was that of the plurality of value spheres and value orientations. But Weber did not introduce this notion in order to deepen the liberal commitment to the formation of non-ascriptive social ties foundational for a consensual social order. For him the idea had more to do with the intractable conflict of the spheres opened up by the modern rationalization of world views and life-contexts, and his own rather formal and socially indeterminate conception of human freedom and meaning. Here his basic insight was that different "life-orders" are structured around different values, and these values in turn structure basic commitments and orientations to life in incompatible ways.[1] On the "polytheism" of values Weber remarked:

> It is really a question not only of alternatives between values but of an irreconcilable death struggle, like that between "God" and the "Devil." Between these, neither relativization nor compromise is possible. At least not in the true sense. There are, of course, as everyone realizes in the course of his life, compromises, both in fact and in appearance, and at every point. In almost every important attitude of real human beings, the value spheres cross and interpenetrate. The shallowness of our routinized daily existence in the most significant sense of the word consists indeed in the fact that the persons who are caught up in it do not become aware, and above all do not wish to become aware, of this partly psychologically, part pragmatically conditioned motley of irreconcilably antagonistic values. They avoid

---

[1] This idea is developed in Weber, "Religious Rejections of the World and their Significance," in *From Max Weber: Essays in Sociology*.

the choice between "God" and the "Devil" and their own ultimate decision as to which of the conflicting values will be dominated by the one, and which by the other.[2]

The model of secular freedom Weber ultimately champions is not only incompatible with a reconciliation of conflict but is not even available to those who take this as an ultimate aim. Rather everything comes down to the challenge for the individual to live up to the fateful nature of this conflict. It is important to see how Weber's sociology of religion provides many of the crucial insights for elaborating the ontology of human autonomy and struggle that underpins his views on politics and individuality.[3]

PERSONALITY AND THE TENSION BETWEEN ETHICS AND POLITICS

The various value-spheres or "life orders"—politics, religion, law, science, economy, art, erotic life—that are mentioned by Weber exhibit not only conflicts with one another, but also represent different and competing standpoints for rationalizing life.[4] Indeed not each sphere may by its own standards be viewed or developed in such a way that rationalization will always take the same form. In some cases rationalization will relate to the external aspects of action connected with material interests, legal rules, conventions or problems of technical or procedural control. On the other hand rationalization may deal with the internal aspects of action, such as personal direction, commitment, the search for meaning and the intrinsic quality of intentional action. Spheres in which rationalization has been most, but not exclusively, applicable to the external situation are those of the economy, law, and science. Those spheres which have been rationalized around the internal conditions of action are those of art, erotic life and systematically developed religious ethics.

---

[2] "The Meaning of 'Ethical Neutrality'", p. 17.

[3] For a similar linkage between these two aspects of Weber's work see the excellent discussion in Rogers Brubaker, *The Limits of Rationality: An Essay on the Social and Moral Thought of Max Weber*, ch. 3.

[4] Weber, *The Protestant Ethic and the Spirit of Capitalism*, p. 78.

But it is the religious sphere which formed the dominant concern of Weber's historical sociology. Religion has pressed its claims in both the external and internal direction. Its earlier manifestations primarily stressed techniques of control such as magic, ritual and particularized codes of obligation sanctioned by divine compensation and punishments. But its later developments have centered around the rationalization of internal demands in connection with faith and (social or personal) ethics. It is the latter aspect that has had the most dynamic impact in the process of Western rationalization. This is largely because the object of ethics has (particularly under the influence of "salvation" religions) become universalized, especially as the focus of religion turned toward an interpretation of the situation of the "sufferer *per se*" as opposed to that of kinship and social hierarchy. The content of ethical action was made into a self-sufficient end as opposed to conformity with a code of moral behaviour. As a result, the objective of ethics becomes detached from interests in "natural relations" which must appear contingent from the point of view of rationalization within religion.[5] Weber even argues that religious rationalization cannot be understood solely by the social or political need to provide an alibi for suffering or worldly injustice, but rather primarily by the independent force of intellectualization which grows from an "inner compulsion to understand the world as a meaningful cosmos and to take up a position toward it."[6]

But the distinctiveness of Western, *cultural* rationalization is also due to the fact that for all the value-spheres, intellectual systematization, or "conscious sublimation," has emphasized each sphere's distinctive intrinsic demands, "thereby letting them drift into those tensions which remain hidden to [religion's] originally naive relation with the external world."[7] However, these tensions come to the fore most decisively as a consequence of religious rationalization which, to simplify Weber's enormously complex account, has to do with separating what one owes to god from what one owes to man. Salvation religions allow ethics to become a sphere specializing in the rational development of personality,

---

[5] "Religious Rejections of the World," pp. 329–30.
[6] *Economy and Society*, vol. 1, p. 499.
[7] "Religious Rejections of the World," p. 328.

organizing behaviour to fulfil intrinsic motivational demands rather than the requirements of external conformity to prescriptions.

This process allows for the specialization of the claims around which religion has been intellectually and ethically rationalized, but is not by itself the source of religion's cultural dynamism in Protestant asceticism which interested Weber. Indeed asceticism and mysticism both incorporate practically rational solutions to the problem of systematizing faith as a part of one's total orientation to life. Asceticism tends to become a more revolutionary rationalizing force since its way of renouncing the "demand that the world conform to religious claims" motivated it to confront the other orders of the world in their own terms.[8] The process of the specifically innovative development of ethical rationalization as it took place in the West promoted a unique development of the individualization of responsibility for one's own state of grace, and the character-forming discipline of the internal demands of religious piety required of the believer. If Weber was centrally concerned with Protestant asceticism it is because these ethical demands were structured so as to lead the believer back into the everyday world in a manner that does not require either a denial, or a fatalistic acceptance, of the religious meaninglessness of mundane interests.

It is well known that Weber claimed that the ethical discipline of the "inner-worldly" ascetic had an elective affinity with the "practical rationalism" of bourgeois capitalism. Weber argues that it was Protestant asceticism, especially that of Calvinism, which made it possible to connect the achievement of religiously sanctioned status with successful, depersonalized instrumental dealings with the persons and forces of this world. The resulting "ethical discipline"—the purpose of which is to revolutionize the "institutional structure" of society—provides a way of overcoming the ethical meaninglessness of the "natural" or "creaturely" world while affirming the world as a proving ground of religious virtue.[9] It was this "ethos" that moved members of influential social strata to become committed to impersonal, *formally* rational institutions such as capitalistic enterprise, the bureaucratic rule of law and procedure, and even aspects of modern science. By contrast,

---

[8] *Economy and Society*, vol. 1, p. 543, 548.

[9] Ibid., pp. 547–8.

the former ethics of brotherly service enjoined believers to account consciously for the state of their souls by directing themselves purely toward an "acosmism of love."[10]

For this ethos the intrinsic value of one's intentions is the only test of virtue which matters. Any abiding interest in worldly consequences is in conflict with seeking a guarantee of salvation through obedience to unconditionally binding moral obligations of Christian love. The history of churchly Christianity is characterized by the routinized dissolution of the religious charisma of the virtuoso. Its individualizing influence is stunted by the demand that believers organize their lives around the stereotyping of action by the maxims of brotherliness or acosmic love. The only pre-Reformation strand of the world-rejecting type to move in the direction of individualist-rationalistic virtuosity was that of monastic asceticism. The monk proved his religious charisma *through* routine, but the direction of this form of practical rationalism was purely acosmic.[11]

Weber evidently wants to show how neither of the latter alternative directions of rationalization could have had an elective affinity with the pattern of individualization that produced the leading social institutions of the modern world. In this regard contemporary theorists of modernization or social evolution see Weber's work on religion, with its focus on the Protestant ethic, as an account of how Western culture could "solve the problem" of integrating ethically meaningful motivation into the spheres of "affectively neutral" social relationships in a way that is necessary for participation in "advanced" socio-economic institutions. But this perspective assumes that Weber's primary interest was to define the structural problems of modernity in evolutionary terms. It therefore neglects his interest in presenting the direction of Western rationalism as a particular way of developing ethics as a proving ground of individuality and personality. He therefore states:

> The Puritan, like every rational type of asceticism, tried to enable a man to maintain and act upon his constant motives, especially those which it taught

---

[10] "Religious Rejections of the World," p. 330.

[11] *The Protestant Ethic*, p. 81.

him itself, against the emotions. In this formal psychological sense of the term it tried to make him into a personality.[12]

The ethical significance of personality, as it is repeated elsewhere in his work, has to do with whether one can live meaningfully. A personality develops through the "consistency of its inner relationship to certain ultimate values and meanings of life, which are turned into purposes and thus into teleologically rational action."[13]

The other available options in religious rationalism may be rational in their own terms, but they lose their developmental significance for shaping a personality-forming, worldly political-economic ethos because they relieve believers of the inherent tension between ethics and the other spheres. The reliance on the traditionalism of church authority limits the degree to which specifically ethical aspects (as opposed to the cultic, ritualistic, magical or contemplative elements) can be translated into systematic worldly personal demands upon the religiously faithful. Moreover, the belief that religion boils down to the injunction toward brotherly service could not form the 'template' of modern individualism. It presupposes that there could be a self-sufficient standpoint from which to test the "intrinsic value" of one's action in the world, and it thereby prevents ethical rationalization from systematically confronting the inherent tension between ethics and the world.[14] And finally, monastic asceticism, though thoroughly rationalistic, assumed that worldly morality had to be opposed rather than made into a proving ground of religious virtuosity.[15]

Contained in this approach is perhaps a model of social evolution, but more definitively an ontology of personality and rational social action which takes life "in its own terms," and recognizes that "the ultimately possible attitudes toward life are irreconcilable."[16] The decisive feature of Protestant asceticism was that it placed a premium upon heroically confronting the "ethical irrationality" of the world and

---

[12] Ibid., p. 119.
[13] *Roscher and Knies*, p. 192.
[14] "Religious Rejections of the World," pp. 338–39.
[15] *The Protestant Ethic*, pp. 80, 119-21.
[16] "Science as a Vocation," in *From Max Weber*, p. 152.

everyday human needs. It does so even at the price of its own irrationality in utilitarian terms. In Weber's sociology the duty to follow god ennobles the search for meaning when believers are left without any rational account of the content of the commands or guarantee that obedience will conform to self-interest. Weber claims that this motif of a *deus absconditus* grew out of the "experience of the irrationality of the world [which] has been the driving force of all religious evolution."[17] He proposes that Calvinism's version of this motif (with its doctrine of predestination) provided a model of ethically meaningful action which did not require flight from the world. The 'vocational' personality formed under the influence of Calvinism refuses to adjust his action—in a merely adaptive way—to everyday needs and, rather, accepts the calling of mastering the everyday world.

Weber does not believe that this attitude can be anchored, or developed as a sustained evolutionary achievement, in the contemporary world. The institutional life of the contemporary world appears to him as a worn-out springboard of cultural innovation that has long since lost its directive power. The world influenced by protestant asceticism and modern science has become "disenchanted" and the victory of capitalism is described by Weber in terms of a spiritless "fate" imposed on modern humanity by its own devices, rather than as an "evolutionary breakthrough" through which mundane activity can be connected with ethical motives.[18] At best, the spiritual conditions of the modern world, while denying individuals a guarantee of ethical meaning through world mastery, present them with a new challenge to create such meaning.

The modern individual knows that the ultimate meaning of one's conduct is not simply 'given,' that it is problematic in its relation to other spheres of meaning, and that the belief in the validity of values cannot be rationally defended. Life is a struggle amongst incommensurable ultimate values which does not so much establish the relativity of values as force the responsible individual to choose between them, which, in our context, means to choose between an orientation to success and an orientation to moral principle. Hence for Weber it makes no sense to say that the rational telos of moral-practical life is the

---

[17] "Politics as a Vocation," p. 123.
[18] *The Protestant Ethic*, p. 181-2.

creation of a society in which individuals would be free to define their own purposes and values. A consistent attempt to reconstruct political life according to the principles of free and rational consent would entail following an "ethic of conviction." It would be animated by a belief in the ideal perfectibility of society as a sphere of moral value, and would therefore have to abandon responsibility for the permanent connection of politics to struggle, conflict and the use of compulsory means. Weber is explicit about the connection of this ethic with the "acosmism of love."[19] By contrast, one who follows an "ethic of responsibility" would be imbued with a greater sense of the tension between ethics and politics.[20] She would be aware that the ultimate ends of action are not subject to rational choice and that the attempt to act in an ethically meaningful manner cannot exempt itself from the potentially ironic implications of political implementation.

In the ethic of responsibility one is, above all, accountable for the "foreseeable consequences" of one's actions rather than for the consistency with which one is oriented to the intrinsic value of the goal. As Rogers Brubaker has put it, the tensions between the value-spheres "force the individual who wishes to consciously guide his life to *choose* between competing definitions of rationality." We cannot avoid "nonrational choice about the very meaning of rationality."[21] Weber does not argue that the spheres of ethics and politics are completely heterogeneous however. Rather he proposes that in politics one is accountable to the discrepancy between ethical demands, and between ideal and reality, in a way that one *need not* be from a rational ethical standpoint.[22] The follower of an ethic of ultimate ends can act consistently so long as she is willing to "leave the outcome to god." But in this case she must forgo the attempt to deal resolutely and creatively with contingent circumstances, conflicts among ethical ideals whose validity cannot be rationally demonstrated,[23] and the unequal capacities

---

[19] "Politics as a Vocation," p. 126.

[20] Ibid., pp. 118–9.

[21] Brubaker, *The Limits of Rationality*, p. 87.

[22] "The Meaning of 'Ethical Neutrality'," pp. 16–17; "Politics as a Vocation," p. 121.

[23] This aspect of the problem of the ethically undecidable content of social and political justice is dealt with in "The Meaning of 'Ethical Neutrality'," pp. 15–16.

of people. Weber insists that the ethic of responsibility also includes the goal of shaping reality according to imperatives that are justified in terms of ultimate values. But politics is more pointedly a question of blending passion with judgement and distance, which requires the subjection of ideal goals, and the realization of human potential, to a "trained relentlessness in viewing the realities of life."[24] The measure of a genuine personality in politics is therefore not a crude Machiavellianism but an intimate awareness of the tragic qualities of action.[25]

POLITICS IN WEBER'S CONCEPT OF MEANING

The foregoing account affords an opportunity to look more closely at Weber's approach to the understanding of meaning. We have already suggested how his socio-cultural investigations were informed by the problem of the rationally autonomous personality. If the puritan sects represented a cultural innovation it was that of giving certain leadership strata the task of stylizing their lives both inwardly and externally as instruments of spiritual development. The early bourgeois life-style can be seen as the result of a purely ethical interpretation of methodical-rational development of conduct, placing a premium upon personal uprightness and an orientation to business-like success. This "value-rational" meaning assigned to success in "purposive-rational" or "economically rational" action was unique precisely because it was devoid of utilitarian significance. It therefore was able to realize possibilities that could only remain latent in previous types of religious rationalization which identified worldly success with a utilitarian attitude. Once it became institutionalized, however, this "vocational" ethos became unhinged from religion by the ultimate reinforcement of utilitarian attitudes under bureaucratic-capitalism.

Talcott Parsons is perhaps most famous for his account of Weber's thought as an alternative to the utilitarian rationalism which distinguished the 19th century liberal tradition of social theory. Parsons claims that Weber's account of the culturally unique combination of value-rational meaning and instrumental activism needs to be fitted into

---

[24] "Politics as a Vocation," pp. 126–27.
[25] Ibid., p. 117.

a better account of how the constitutive elements of action and social order can be made intelligible only with reference to the operation of normative beliefs and ideal motives. Compensating for Weber's failure to emphasise the constitutive normative element in meaningful action, Parsons believes he can demonstrate how such motives are still operative in an individualistic society.[26]

From Parsons' perspective Weber exaggerates the independent importance of hierarchical power and bureaucracy, as compared to the value system of pluralism and collegial models of authority. In this way Weber could not envisage any path of modernization other than an inevitable undermining of the once promising normative culture of individualism.[27] But Parsons argues that if Weber had properly understood the kind of solidarity that corresponds to legal-rational authority, he could have shown how the "hierarchical" aspect of power is attenuated by more effective patterns of citizenship and a normative culture which sanctions the responsible use of power and influence. Parsons tries to show how the assumption of an inevitable discrepancy between ideal and reality is not so much false, but the result of a false *problem*. The bureaucratization of authority is not a fatal flaw of modern society, but rather a misfiring of a social system that otherwise makes it possible to institutionalize an effective normative culture of responsible individualism.

Weber was perhaps subject to a nostalgia for the great and unique motivational convergence of ideal and material interests that he believed distinguished early bourgeois culture. At the very least, the framework of his pre-theoretical commitments led him to investigate the consequences and possibilities of the search for meaning in an era in which that unity had been sundered. The intellectual frameworks of enlightenment liberalism, Marxism and theories of social evolution and progress would not suffice. From his standpoint these perspectives privilege the rational foundations of theoretical and practical ideals at the expense of recognizing the contextual relativity of social and historical understand-

---

[26] These points are at the core of Parsons' "Introduction" to Max Weber, *The Theory of Social and Economic Organization*.

[27] Talcott Parsons, "On Building Social System Theory: A Personal History," *Social Systems and the Evolution of Action Theory*, pp. 54–56.

ing itself and the ephemeral value of the concepts used in a science that studies meaning-constituted action.[28]

Weber himself, of course, was committed to advancing a determinate theoretical approach of his own. The central task in social science, he argues, is to understand meaning since intelligible meaning distinguishes every form of social reality as a context of human development, marked by conscious striving and identifiably human intentionality. Weber devoted his famous "methodological" essays to showing the extent to which an "interpretive" social science can be considered a rational tool for understanding the meaning-elements underlying effective contexts of human development. But he also stated that how one constructs a problem of human development depends upon one's "value-interests." To cultivate interpretive judgement one must keep in mind the individuality of historical phenomena rather than their evolutionary significance. Social scientists have no normative criteria outside of those provided by "ideal types." These ideal types are purely hypothetical ascriptions of meaning used for distinguishing what is rational in one context from what is rational in another context, or for distinguishing some imputed model of rationality from the actual course of behaviour. The validity assigned to one's *choice* of theoretical model is intrinsically related to a concrete way of 'lending the world significance' and therefore reflects one's sense of the fate of the waning or emergent context within which one is placed.[29] To this extent there can be no recourse to ideally rational foundations, or the discovery of univocal patterns of social development.

Weber's sociological analysis of Western rationalism was the means by which he articulated his implicit philosophical position regarding the "limits of rationality" in Brubaker's sense. This theme is as conspicuous in his "substantive" sociology as it is in his theory of scientific rationality. Sheldon Wolin argues that the way the modern scientist must confront meaninglessness is structurally similar to the subjective

---

[28] On this point in relation to the problems of concept and reality in Marxism and other approaches which focus on "economically relevant" phenomena see Weber, "Objectivity," pp. 65ff.

[29] For these points see especially Ibid., pp. 81, 107, 111.

stance of the Protestant hero.[30]	Wolin adds that this was felt by Weber to be a challenge that requires scientists to deal with the problem of meaning in political terms.	Indeed, the lesson of Weber's sociology of religion is that the search for religious meaning could not undertake the task of overcoming the meaninglessness of the world *in worldly terms*, without going beyond itself.	In "Science as a Vocation" Weber proposes that the post-religious moral seriousness of the social scientist depends upon how well she can highlight the "necessity of... choice" inhabiting all practical-political life.[31]	Political activity illuminates the existential problem facing anyone who tries to live a meaningful life, and this is revealed in a distinctive way at the limits of scientific knowledge.

Here, at least, Weber places the emphasis on the recognition of the *necessity* to choose, not on the routine *subjectivism* of choice.	He is evidently trying to show how, in the modern age, personality might once again become a test of moral seriousness, even though such an attitude can only be expressed at the level of an individual's calling or vocation in the sphere of specialization and the modern division of labour.	When Weber states that life is a series of ultimate decisions,[32] he is saying that the recognition of the conflict among the contending gods or value-standpoints can be borne only by a personality expressing itself in potentially political terms.	This means that the individual can remain a personality only in so far as she strives to forge her ideal motives, goals and worldly responsibilities into a consistent whole, never separating values from success, yet realizing that "moral paradoxes" will always assert themselves.	Only from the standpoint of genuinely political activity can one gain the best understanding of how the possibility of meaning occurs against the background of meaninglessness.	If science is a form of political activity for Weber—as Wolin argues—it is because he felt that science can return us to the problem of choice in a world in which choice regularly loses its connection to character and personality.[33]

---

[30] Sheldon Wolin "Max Weber: Legitimation, Method and the Politics of Theory."
[31] "Science as a Vocation," p. 151.
[32] "The Meaning of 'Ethical Neutrality'," p. 18.
[33] Wolin, "Max Weber: Legitimation, Method and the Politics of Theory,", p. 409;

It was therefore Weber's conception of the "existential" problem of genuinely meaningful human action—not any spurious cultural pessimism—which caused him to be preoccupied with the discrepancy between ideal and reality in action and understanding.[34] Awareness of the tragic qualities of action was therefore the precondition of both politics *and* social theory. Weber often accounted for this in the way he qualified the demands of his sociological theory. He was concerned to show how social reality does not only express the way people engage in purposive activity and their search for meaning, but also how they adjust to reality more passively, through blind impulse and habit, coercion, motives of expediency or fideistic commitments to values. Moreover, Weber believed that sociology is "interpretive," that its task was to understand the meaning people assign to their actions; but he also insisted that it must recognize "[l]ife with its irrational reality."[35] For Weber the meaning of action, or the systems of meaning in a society, can only be rationally elucidated up to a point. This is because there is a boundary between meaning and meaninglessness in all of social reality which is not simply there prior to our actions but is made and remade by our actions.

Social scientists cannot try to impose a rational meaning upon the world or upon other people, but neither can they anticipate an ideally

---

See also later in his discussion (p. 419) where Wolin argues that judgements about what is worth knowing, judgements of value relevance in Weber's terms, are akin to political action. They represent "the moment of freedom for the social scientist when he registers his affirmations, when he exchanges the settled routines of inquiry for the risks of action."

[34] Jeffrey Alexander acknowledges the similarities of Weber's analysis of human personality and freedom to that of Sartre's existentialism. But he proposes that this starting point is for Weber a result of his understanding of "historical conditions rather than human ontology." But Alexander does not consider that Sartre's philosophy may itself be a response to historical conditions, or that Weber's understanding of the 'problem' in the light of which he views sociohistorical developments may be informed by philosophical ideas such as those of Nietzsche. His ultimate qualification of Weber's "pessimism" rests on accepting elements of Parsons' view of modern society with its idea that "differentiation, depersonalization and secularization can lead to flexibility and adaptiveness rather than to discipline and rigid control." ("Individuation and Domination," in *Max Weber, Rationality and Modernity*, pp. 198, 204); See also ch. 3 below.

[35] "Objectivity," p. 111.

constituted world in which everyone would be free to determine their lives according to meanings that they have consciously chosen. In this connection Martin Albrow has observed that, for an interpretive social science, a rational interpretation of meaning is inapplicable to the goal of perfecting shared understanding.[36] Ideal types are concessions to the impossibility of ideal communication. Indeed, scientists are responsible not for resolving the questions that make meaning problematic but solely for making possible "accurate"[37] communication. Anyone who tries to understand meaning cannot assume that there are practically independent or neutral means for establishing what will count as an adequate ground for meaning or successful communication: "In [Weber's] terms the understanding which people share of events in the world and of each other is always a matter of assumptions for practical purposes and never grounded in an ideal."[38]

Nevertheless, for Weber the very concept of meaningful action presupposes the potential for rationality in the sense of conscious accountability for intelligible motives, beliefs, purposes, responses to situations and the means for implementing them. In this connection Wolfgang Schluchter is correct when he states that "the *conceptually presumed* consistency of personality is a kind of transcendental precondition of interpretive sociology."[39] This means that the subjective motivation of a meaningful action is intelligible as a conscious, goal-oriented selection among possibilities rather than as an outcome of constraint (in cases of material necessity or coercion) or the influence of natural drives and instincts. Many have criticized Weber's theory of social action, and its assumption that the teleologically effective social actor is the ultimate source of meaning in social life. However, in the present context, we can best address these criticisms by turning to the rather complex employment of Weber's theory of meaning in his political sociology.

---

[36] Martin Albrow, *Max Weber's Construction of Social Theory*, pp. 224–25.

[37] Levine, *The Flight from Ambiguity*, p. 153.

[38] Albrow, *Max Weber's Construction of Social Theory*, p. 225.

[39] Wolfgang Schluchter, "Value-Neutrality and the Ethic of Responsibility," in Guenther Roth and Wolfgang Schluchter, *Max Weber's Vision of History*, p. 73.

The Inherence of Power in
Social Relationships

Weber's theory of meaningful action is constructed around the idea that one is more subjectively free—in the sense of possessing a capacity for effective character development and autonomy—the more she adopts a rational orientation. Since Weber is interested in subjectively meaningful action he does not confine himself to the kind of rationality that characterizes the negatively free actor, who is free of external authority and control and who responds to material and social conditions out of enlightened self-interest. In sociological terms the rational loosening of action from tradition and prejudice is a condition for "deliberate adaptation to situations in terms of self-interest"[40] but not an independently important source of meaning for subjectively free and rational actors. Hence the potential for rational action applies also to the total purposive life-orientation and personality, intellectual understandings or value-orientation, and therefore may include a diversity of possible ideal-typical meanings.

In accord with this understanding action may have a rational meaning either 1) from the standpoint of the ultimate values one's action serves, in which case it is "value rational", or 2) from the standpoint of responding to the conditions of one's action by selecting available means and considering the probable consequences of action, in which case it is "instrumentally rational." The first type, value rational action, is action as it is "determined by a conscious belief in the value for its own sake of some ethical, aesthetic, religious or other form of behaviour, independently of its prospects of success." Weber specifically states that, as an ideal type, one who acts in a value rational manner experiences certain demands as binding on her, and tries to order her life so as to fulfil them for their own sake. Value rational action may therefore be viewed as "irrational" from the standpoint of action oriented toward success, but not from its own standards which may be developed in a systematic and consistent way.[41] Of course, in his portrayal of modern developments, Weber is famous for having shown the 'cash value' of his

---

[40] *Economy and Society*, vol. 1, p. 30.
[41] Ibid., pp. 24–6.

analytic categories, that is, for showing that the modern bureaucratic institutionalization of instrumentally rational action tends to work against the chance of adapting to, or mastering, situations in terms of value-rational meaning.

The potential for rational action is lowest in the case of the "traditional" and the "affectual" orientations, the two "borderline" types of action-orientation. The former refers to the case in which action is a matter of "ingrained habit" while in the latter it is based on emotional attachment or heartfelt devotion. Whether or not such conduct will count as meaningful, or potentially rational, depends upon whether the rules, standards or leading persons by which it is motivated can, for ideal-type purposes, be said to constitute ideals or formulas according to which one's life can be consciously and deliberately ordered. On the other hand it is not considered meaningful when traditional or affectual motives operate like purely psychological stimuli, as in the case of subjection to behavioural inducements like fear or in the case of crowd-behaviour.[42]

It is well known that whatever unacknowledged value-judgements may be implicit in Weber's use of the terms 'meaning' or 'rationality' they stem from the basic assumptions about relevant human capacities that frame his thought. In this respect we can take note of the objections made by Bryan Turner and others about the evaluative nature of Weber's categories themselves and his attempt to distinguish human beings by their capacity for noble motives.[43] However, Weber's concept of meaning-constituted behaviour is clearly at the root of his conception of realizing personality through politics. His discussion of a social relationship, the first stage of his political sociology, is built up from his starting point which posits the orientation toward meaning as the distinguishing mark of agency. He states that a social relationship exists when the orientation toward meaning involves taking account of the actions of others. It therefore requires the judgement of a "probability" that people will assign meaning to their action in a certain way: that they will be motivated by the material interests or needs of their

---

[42] Ibid., pp. 23, 25.

[43] For one of the best discussions of Weber's philosophical anthropology see Brubaker, *The Limits of Rationality*, ch. 4.

situation, the intrinsic values to be implemented, or the success with which they can use and organize means to achieve given ends.[44]

Weber claims that one can still speak of a meaning-constituted social relationship when "parties associate different meanings to their actions" so long as, at the level of "expectation," a "mutual orientation" can be maintained.[45] This is why Weber refused to identify an independently important, or 'ideal' source of meaning in society such as consensus, emotional bonds, shared values or calculation of self-interest. In fact if one tries to trace the quality of a social relationship to some ideal element, such as a consensus among rational partners or a harmony of interests, one risks ignoring the actual meaning element of the relationship which may be different for the various participants who may act out of a sense of duty or expediency or otherwise. There is therefore an inevitable contingency underlying every meaning-constituted social relationship since whether one is an observer or participant the relationship involves a purposive pursuit of actions, or adoption of expectations, oriented to the expectations or actions of others. The assumption of a "probability of action" is the basis not only for participating in a social relationship but also for making observations about its character. This probability of action is contingent because it depends upon subjective attitudes, intentions, choices, and beliefs that may be voluntarily or deliberately pursued in response to the voluntary or deliberate actions of others.

In light of this element of contingency—as well as the variety of individual orientations and motives—rules or "maxims" are often the common focus of people in a social relationship.[46] When rules have the "prestige of being considered binding" Weber speaks of a "legitimate order." And when the "belief in the existence of a legitimate order" is a motivational basis for a probability of action then the "order" is said to be "valid." Hence a valid order is a meaningful part of a social relationship when at least some people regard the order as binding and when others take this into account in their actions whatever "other

---

[44] *Economy and Society*, vol. 1, pp. 26–28.

[45] Ibid., p. 26–7.

[46] Albrow, *Max Weber's Construction of Social Theory*, p. 163.

sources of conformity" may also exist.[47]   One can never say that an order's validity depends exclusively upon the possibility of discovering rational grounds for the claim to legitimacy since conformity, or the expectation of conformity, may be motivationally oriented to the existence of laws or conventions and the sanctions attached to them, or even habituation to them.   Indeed, given the empirical nature of the concept of validity, only the "stability" of the order, not its legitimacy, is greater the more one ascends along the series: expediency, habit, rational persuasiveness, bindingness (or duty).

But this theoretical complexity only attests to the fact that criteria of validity in sociology are different, and more gradually shaded than they are in juristic thought and normative theories of social order.   The sociological validity of an order depends upon the probability that a given interpretation of the meaning of the order will determine certain actions.[48]   The rules may be adhered to either because they are considered right, intrinsically compelling and perhaps ideally justifiable, or because of considerations of expediency.   The distinction between motives and reasons is therefore fluid when it comes to making the legitimacy of an order intelligible.   In juristic thought, however, rationally justifiable rules and principles must be sharply distinguished from other kinds of motives as the basis of validity.   The sociological validity of an order may be established whether its standards are regarded as intrinsically compelling or whether it is regarded from the standpoint of the "external" interest situation to which legal or conventional rules appeal.[49]   At this point in Weber's analysis the meaning-orientation of political order is a reflection of the complexity of empirical motivations and constitutive meanings in society, with no priority given to the justification of normative claims, beliefs, interest-based conformity, and emotional attitudes.

In a later section of *Economy and Society* the *claim* to legitimacy is discussed in a way that differs from the earliest sections I have been reviewing where the analysis of the *guarantee* of legitimacy is prominent.   The later sections appeal more exclusively to the "beliefs", on the

---

[47] *Economy and Society*, vol. 1, p. 31.

[48] Ibid., p. 32.

[49] "Politics as a Vocation," p. 79.

part of actors, in the validity of the order.[50] Here actors who treat the order as worthy of acceptance "ascribe" its validity to either tradition, revelation (or an exemplary phenomenon), the discovery of an ultimate value or the rational enactment of the positive legal order. Aside from Weber's remarks that these are only "pure types" it is natural to ask why he at one point defines legitimacy by including more utilitarian motives and at another point only in terms of beliefs in ideal claims to validity.[51] In addition, one might challenge Weber as to why the ascription of validity to the binding claims of a legal rational order is independent of whether that order is imposed or based on consent. And finally is Weber not guilty of inconsistency with his own view of the complexity of meaning-constituted social relationships when he argues that a social relationship like "the state" must be defined *exclusively* in terms of the means specific to it rather than by its ends?[52]

It is well-known that all of these problems come to the fore in Weber's construction of his typology of legitimate domination. Here he insists that the "inner justifications" of authority provide the motives for obedience that are essential to organized power. In these sections the meaning element underlying the compliance of the 'ruled' is more narrowly construed; what counts is that their interest in obeying an authority takes the form of an inner belief in the claim upon which it is ideally based.

> The validity of the claims to legitimacy may be based on:
> 1. Rational grounds—resting on the belief in the legality of enacted rules and the right of those elevated to authority under such rules to issue commands (legal authority).
> 2. Traditional grounds—resting on the established belief in the sanctity of immemorial traditions and the legitimacy of those exercising authority under them (traditional authority); or finally,
> 3. Charismatic grounds—resting on devotion to the exceptional sanctity, heroism or exemplary character of an individual person, and of the normative patterns or order revealed or ordained by him (charismatic authority)[53]

---

[50] *Economy and Society*, vol. 1, pp. 36, 212ff.
[51] Merquior, *Rousseau and Weber*, p. 93.
[52] "Politics as a Vocation," p. 77–78.
[53] *Economy and Society*, vol. 1, p. 215.

Why is "value rationality", in which the meaning element is the intrinsic value of the goal to be achieved by the political organization, excluded as grounds for accepting its authority? Weber apparently believed that natural law foundations—which he called "the purest type of legitimacy based on value-rationality"[54]—ignore the ineluctable authoritarian substance of politics and the resulting tension between ethics and politics. But why is it in the very nature of political legitimacy that it can never be based on a rational commitment to socially valid ideals? Why, in other words, does Weber's political sociology fail to acknowledge the possibility of a rational consensual order of the type required by the ideals of liberal democracy?

To the extent that Weber himself provides an *overt* justification of his approach he refers to the need for any system of legitimate domination to achieve internal support and to organize its power effectively:

> What is important is the fact that in a given case the particular claim to legitimacy is to a significant degree and according to its type treated as "valid"; that this fact confirms the position of the persons claiming authority and that it helps to determine the choice of means of its exercise.[55]

But here Weber never addresses the apparent inconsistency between his theory of the multidimensional nature of social action and the unidimensionality of legitimate domination. In this connection Martin Barker has shown that the answer to our question is that there is only apparent inconsistency, and that on closer inspection Weber's failure to carry value-rationality over into the typology of legitimate domination, stems from his very conception of social action itself.

We can summarize Barker's argument in the terms we have already developed.[56] Weber argues that we can define meaningful action with reference to the actor's subjective freedom and potential for rationality. The potentially rational agent is one who orients herself to an open field of possibilities in a conscious and goal-directed way, taking account of how her situation is conditioned and the available means for responding

---

[54] Ibid., p. 37.
[55] Ibid., p. 214.
[56] Martin Barker, "Kant as a Problem for Weber," pp. 224-45.

to those conditions or realizing her goals. Since the choice of goals is subjective the only way an actor can rationally coordinate her goals with those of others is by treating others as potential conditions or means to her ends. However, given the contingency of social relationships, one can only act rationally to the extent that one expects others to want to determine their actions and beliefs on the basis of their own definitions of their goals and their capacity to realize them. My freedom, in a social relationship of any complexity, will depend upon imposing motives and meanings on others in a way that could be instrumentally effective in influencing their contingently free goal-orientation. As Barker characterizes Weber's conception, "the power relation is therefore the natural relation among men and women."[57]

Barker shows that, from the standpoint of Weber's theory of action, organized power is the basis for developing the most rational orientation in a social relationship. Indeed, he defines power with a view to the contingency of social relationships, that is, as the probability of realizing one's goals in spite of the possible resistance of others, and no matter what those goals are or what that probability rests upon.[58] Of course for Weber "domination" is power supplemented by the means of organization and discipline. This requires a distinction between political domination and other kinds. Although domination in general signifies the exercise of a "power of command" over others, its resources can be those of rewards, knowledge, expert qualifications, property, status inequality, control over the means of production and control over the means of violence. But specifically political or "legitimate" domination is to be distinguished from other kinds of domination and from power itself, whose 'ultimate' means is violence. What makes domination "legitimate" is not only the probability that compliance will take place, but that it will take place "as if the ruled had made the content of the command the maxim of their conduct for its own sake."[59] The factor

---

[57] Ibid., p. 242; Niklas Luhmann regrets that, despite Weber's insight into the contingency of social action, it did not permit him to disentangle the conception of law from the concept of domination. On this, and a particularly good formulation of Weber's account of the contingency problem see Niklas Luhmann, *A Sociology of Law*, pp. 16-17.

[58] *Economy and Society*, vol. 1, p. 53.

[59] *Economy and Society,* vol. 2, p. 946.

of organization that makes this possible is neither coercion nor the control of resources (even though violence is the ultimate instrument of organized power in the modern state) but rather the capacity to make subjection to power indistinguishable from the choice of certain actions and beliefs by the subject acted upon.

Max Weber is not the only theorist to argue that power is most effective when the types of action it makes possible result from the freedom of agents to choose their beliefs and attachments. Murray Edelman is perhaps the most noteworthy recent political scientist to show how the process of political legitimation depends upon this ambiguity.[60] Power, he says, is exercised more easily by the ambiguous qualities taken on by the terms "freedom" and "rationality" when used in "hortatory language". In some respects Weber's and Edelman's work converge with that of Michel Foucault who proposes that power works by concealing the actual situation of power, including its effort to cultivate useful people, behind the nominal attachment to independently persuasive ideals such as reform. At its most basic level, Foucault's definition of power as an action performed upon another's capacity to act captures the essence of Weber's less explicit conception.[61]

PRE-EMPTING LIBERAL DEMOCRACY

We have alluded to Weber's view that only an ethics that takes account of the "hard realities" of politics can sustain a genuinely autonomous individual in a secular age. But again this trades upon a conception that remains implicit in his basic approach to action, namely that a certain way of organizing power—controlling the meanings and alternatives that will shape the expectations of others—provides the most rational

---

[60] Murray Edelman, *The Symbolic Uses of Politics*, pp. 134ff.

[61] Foucault writes: "In itself the exercise of power is not violence; nor is it a consent which, implicitly, is renewable. It is a total structure of actions brought to bear upon possible actions; it incites, it induces, it seduces it makes easier or more difficult; in the extreme case it constrains or forbids absolutely; it is nevertheless always a way of acting upon an acting subject or acting subjects by virtue of their acting or being capable of action [or upon their 'freedom' as Foucault puts it later]." ("The Subject and Power," in Hubert Dreyfuss and Paul Rabinow, *Michel Foucault: Beyond Structuralism and Hermeneutics,* p. 221.)

orientation that can be adopted in a social relationship. This kind of control can only be effective to the extent to which it is not recognized, or regarded as something else, by those subject to it. Weber clearly shares Nietzsche's belief that the world is not, and can never be, rational or meaningful in itself. Consequently, if one wants to act rationally or meaningfully one cannot guide one's actions by the goal of shaping social reality in such a way that no one will be a means to someone else's ends. Nor can we even try to build a society in which the conceptions of action and freedom that do embody genuinely shared hopes will not be overtaken by the means for realizing them.

In this connection Barker faults Weber for rejecting the Kantian lineage of his conceptions of autonomy and personality in favour of a Nietzschean emphasis on creating meaning for others to live by as a way of overcoming contingency:

> For Kant,...transcendental hope was a prerequisite for the meaningfulness of morality. By subversion of one piece of this argument, Weber brings pessimism crashing down on his head....The world is beyond human understanding. There are only versions of the world that allow us to survive.
>
> The distinction between noumenon and phenomenon, which is at the heart of the Kantian scheme of things, sets up the possibility of a rational kingdom of ends. It is missing in Weber. Everything is phenomena. All we have for purposes of understanding are useful fictions; and that is all we have for living. The best that we can do is to achieve some form of realization of our limitations. In Kant, the noumenal world is a beacon of inviting effort; in Weber, it isn't worth trying.[62]

But in the eyes of other commentators Nietzsche and Weber can be saved from their own pre-emptive rejection of liberal democratic ideals. According to Mark Warren, Weber's "ethically significant sense of politics"[63] actually affords the basis of a liberal democratic critique of the rarification of politics and the expropriation of politics by ruling elites. To explain Weber's shortcomings, however, Warren points to the fact that once he had characterized bureaucracy as both irresistible

---

[62] Barker, "Kant as a Problem for Weber," pp. 241–42.
[63] Warren, "Max Weber's Liberalism for a Nietzschean World," p. 36.

and politically stultifying Weber was compelled to rarefy politics, locating it only in the lives of those with enough courage to create meaning. According to Warren, however, Weber can also be used to show how the ideal of moral autonomy itself requires orientation to a world without "transcendental hope." Weber was right to insist that morality cannot be made meaningful for a rationally autonomous person except by recognizing its connection to politics. Virtue in politics is characterized by the maturity and honesty with which one takes responsibility for the always imperfect linkage between ideals and their consequences.[64]   But, following Warren, Weber could have said that the capacity to meet this challenge of a secularized, disenchanted world is the very point of enlightenment and the advantage of liberal democracy. In light of their "social ontology," Weber and Nietzsche contend that human excellence and moral seriousness can only be realized through a politics of domination. This implies that the moral goals of liberal democracy may only be salvaged in nominal terms, that is, as a contingent means of utilizing or foregrounding the qualities of some distinctive human form or "*Typus Mensch*." They dismiss the possibility that the very ideals of liberal democracy may also be indispensable for learning which of those qualities are worth promoting.[65]

Most of the remainder of this study will focus on thinkers who in differing ways address themselves to the retreat from liberal democracy implicitly or explicitly suggested by Weber, as well as by Nietzsche. There can be no doubt that Weber's central concern as a political thinker was with the "quality of human beings" produced under given conditions and that the liberal democracy of his day appeared to him to have neglected this question altogether. Whether Weber was right to deny the promise of liberal democratic institutions and the possibility of social freedom—and to build this into his analytic framework as a sociologist—is at least debatable, but his attempt to find a convergence between the themes of personality, meaning and politics remains a great challenge to those who would rehabilitate this promise. For him genuine politics is only possible when value choices are seen as ultimate decisions, and the quality with which one makes and lives by one's

---

[64] Ibid.

[65] This point is also made by Merquior, *Rousseau and Weber*, p. 221.

ultimate decisions is a test of human dignity and freedom that cannot be disconnected from politics.

It may be that Weber would have had either to reject or reconstruct the framework of Enlightenment thought in order to address adequately the ambiguities of contemporary conceptions of 'rationality' and 'freedom'. I will look at Habermas' project of reconstruction below. Now, however, I will turn to Alasdaire MacIntyre, who claims that the thought of both Nietzsche and Weber actually reflects the bankrupt foundations of liberal-Enlightenment morality. According to MacIntyre they are mere symptoms of the disease they are trying to cure.

Chapter Three

LIBERALISM AS A MORAL
TRADITION: VICE AS VIRTUE?

We have seen how Max Weber's social theory casts doubt on whether the liberal goal of rationalizing society can be developed in a way that is consistent with a normatively grounded politics. Weber suggests that the perspective of liberalism can no longer offer conceptions of social order and freedom that can stand as independently important sources of ethical meaning and value. This argument derives in part from his insight into the socially indeterminate freedom of individuals. But the tension between his perspective and that of liberalism is primarily driven by his account of the developmental paradoxes of the "specific" rationalism of modern culture. Hence Weber's scepticism toward the moral foundations of liberalism is rarely couched in terms of the method and style of moral and political philosophy. Nevertheless contemporary philosophers have had to confront his view that Western culture has tied itself to a course of rationalization distinguished by the tension between ethics and the other spheres, and that out of this has emerged a dualism between the goods of individuality and those of power and organization. It is the task of this chapter to begin to find alternatives to Weber's social theory in contemporary debates in political philosophy.

ON THE THEORETICAL AND PRACTICAL
FAILURE OF LIBERALISM

According to Weber, once the rationalization of administration and capitalist enterprise had been institutionalized in the contemporary world the vocational depersonalization of conduct could no longer provide a proving ground for the individual's commitment to the "highest spiritual and cultural values."[1] The depersonalization of authority and power could express a commitment to both substantive and formal rationality only so long as a religiously sanctified sense of duty and worldly activism supported the inward drive to bring ethics into the world in a unique manner. Now, however, the growth of depersonalization has come to represent a mere functional imperative linked to the increasingly generalized use of standardized and calculable procedure in law, administration, rational methods of capital accounting and shop and factory discipline. Weber agreed with Marx that one outcome of formally rational economic organization is that human labour becomes abstract so that it becomes "rational" to measure it by the same standards as the other categories of factor inputs. In this way, the disciplined subjection of individuals to impersonal rules no longer frees mundane activity for ethical interpretation.[2] In fact, substantive irrationality has become a normal concomitant of formal rationality. At most Weber can recommend the adoption of an "ethics of responsibility" which requires a certain forbearance toward the demands of the life order within which one is placed. Weber suggests that the guilt-ridden character of such forbearance in the contemporary world is a kind of negative counterpart to the life of the Puritan who could still relate his search for meaning to "some impenetrable divine rationality."[3]

Weber's work is marked by pessimism about developments in modern culture which have made it harder to elaborate a coherent view of the authentic practical substance of human freedom and reason. Accordingly, he speaks of the difficult challenge of making these ideals flourish in the "infertile soil" of modern conditions.[4] In many respects, Weber's conception of "disenchantment" is meant to correspond to what Nietzsche called the "death of god." Both thinkers propose that religious rationalism has created a world in which the commitment to objective values can no longer be justified in religious terms, that is, by the

---

[1] *The Protestant Ethic*, p. 182.

[2] Hennis, *Max Weber: Essays in Reconstruction*, p. 92.

[3] *Economy and Society*, vol. 1, p. 576.

[4] "Prospects for Democracy in Tsarist Russia," in W.G. Runciman, ed., *Weber: Selections in Translation*, p. 283.

intrinsic meaning they give to human choices, struggles and suffering. Weber's concept of "personality" is developed according to the essentially Nietzschean idea that we must create such meaning as individuals.[5] Yet Weber always gives a sociological twist to the Nietzschean background of his thought. He points out that modern institutions operate more and more by enforcing adaptation to functional requirements rather than responsibility for them. Despairing over his own nation's castration of politics, he observed a tendency to divide stewardship of the culture between dilettantes on the one side, and bureaucrats on the other. This is why Weber deplored the politics of the "last man" in Nietzsche's sense and often echoed the latter's call for leadership.

This theme of the crisis of authority has been picked up by later theorists who have analyzed it as one of the central structural problems of liberal Enlightenment culture. Daniel Bell, for example, has noted that the decline of bourgeois responsibility in favour of a morally unrestrained adaptation to the functional requirements of growth and corporate market strategy is characteristic of one side of the fate of modernity. Here the loss of protestant asceticism transforms economic rationalism in a consumerist direction. The values of liberalism have been confined to the political sphere, but have withdrawn from the economic sphere where the coincidence between the ideology of consumer sovereignty and the imperatives of corporate power do not permit a coherent ideological stance.[6] The post-traditional nature of contemporary liberalism legitimizes hedonism in the sphere of "modernist" culture. Bell argues that this is structurally compatible with the economic imperatives of late-capitalism even though the official culture remains anxious about the disdain for utilitarian attitudes in the 'cultural' spheres of leisure and art.

According to Bell, the "disjunction of realms" has led to a loss of legitimacy for modern ideals, and a fragmentation of self for modern individuals. The conflict between an economy justified as a source of rationally efficient organization and cultural modernism justified in the name of expressive autonomy is a particularly ironic one since the

---

[5] Friedrich Nietzsche, *The Gay Science*, no. 301.
[6] Daniel Bell, *The Cultural Contradictions of Capitalism*, p. 79.

modern economy exploits expanded discretion in the pursuit of individual self-definition while it refuses responsibility for the loss of moral bonds and restraints.[7] For its part modernist art exploits the spiritual vacuum, installing the rootless and ephemeral event as the most authentic avenue for autonomous values in culture. Ironically this radical experimentalism, posing as a cultural ascent, has time and again established itself as a parallel to consumer capitalism rather than an antidote to its discontents. But Bell's answer is to have us restore the integrative power of religion to the modern world. However his adherence to social modernization, in the form of a secular differentiated society, becomes implausible at best since it fails to resolve the tensions and disjunctions he describes.[8] The cultural conservatism he recommends is in flat contradiction with his affirmation of the liberal separation between the public good and the freedom of the private sphere.

Alasdaire MacIntyre has displayed a keen sense of the exemplary nature of the problems of social legitimacy and modern selfhood which Bell has identified while avoiding the *prima facia* implausibility of the latter's proposed solution. In his famous work, *After Virtue*, MacIntyre places the blame for the incoherence of liberal-enlightenment culture squarely on the shoulders of the conception of moral reasoning that underpins its philosophical project. He argues that the Weberian features of modern society contain lessons about the faulty foundations of modern ethical thought. In MacIntyre's view, Weber alerts us to the

> bifurcation of the contemporary social world into the realm of the organizational in which ends are taken to be given and not available for rational scrutiny and a realm of the personal in which judgement and debate about values are central factors, but in which no rational resolution of issues is available.[9]

According to MacIntyre Weber belongs to the positivist tradition which

[7] Ibid., pp. 83–4.

[8] For an account of Bell's inconsistency along these lines see John O'Neill, "Religion and Postmodernism: The Durkheimian Bond in Bell and Jameson", in *After the Future: Postmodern Times and Places*, pp. 285–89.

[9] Alasdaire MacIntyre, *After Virtue*, 2nd ed., pp. 34–5.

asserts that our conflicting responses to moral-evaluative questions cannot be solved by reason. More specifically, this points to a crisis in moral reasoning associated with "emotivism." The emotivist holds that moral arguments are ultimately expressions of what we approve or disapprove, so that all moral justification can be nothing more that an attempt to achieve power or influence over others. It is merely our desires that lead us to prefer one state of affairs over another, and these desires are not themselves subject to moral deliberation or legitimate constraint. MacIntyre's main point is that the reigning emotivist assumptions of our culture only discreetly underlie contemporary moral discourse. They are openly exemplified, however, in modern forms of selfhood and sociological accounts of the non-rational foundations of rationality. As he puts it, only by exposing the discrepancy between the "meaning" and the "use" of modern morality can one dramatize the failure of liberalism and its moral culture. This discrepancy, he argues, is not caused by our deviance from Enlightenment liberalism, but rather by that very tradition itself.[10]

MacIntyre's account of the emotivism underlying modern culture is ingenious. Emotivists have non-moral expectations from morality. Hence it is not surprising that an emotivist culture would invest a peculiarly modern figure like the therapist with so much authority. An "emotivist self" needs to determine whether it is in her interest to have certain desires and what are the ultimate consequences of acting on them. In other words, she may ask whether her desires must be adjusted to reality (including the expectations and beliefs of others) or whether reality must be adjusted to our desires. Utilitarian morality, it turns out, is specifically tailored to these questions, and it legitimizes our reliance on morally neutral, impersonal rules for determining how best to order or realize a given set of ends. From the point of view of utilitarianism there are no pre-existing criteria for a rational social order since the rationality of all social rules can be judged by how well, and with what consequences, they can be used to gain access to personal or organizational goods with commensurable value. In this way the dominance of two central character-types in our society—the

---

[10] Ibid., pp. 19–22, 55ff.

bureaucratic manager and the therapist—attest to the heritage of utilitarian morality.

The principles of utilitarianism appear to conflict with the perspective of Kantian autonomy, even though each approach claims to be rational and possess universal validity. From both perspectives the belief in the capacity to establish universal principles on the basis of a liberation from tradition determines the "meaning" of moral claims in modernity. But the "use" of morality is quite different.[11] The claims of utilitarianism have 'force' only when our desire for certain ends can be translated into a rational calculation of self-interest and when the organization of the means for achieving our ends can be informed by the knowledge of "morally neutral facts" about the world. This clearly rests on a fiction, namely that all of our activity and striving has the same kind of purpose—to maximize pleasure and minimize pain.[12] Morality is therefore nothing other than a faith in reason to discover a neutral instrument for optimally realizing the most purposes of the most people by manipulating the rules governing, restricting or promoting striving or activity.

What is distinctive about the claims of utilitarian morality is that they can only carry conviction among those who have an interest in legitimizing claims to bureaucratic authority. Utilitarianism can only think of morality in terms of one kind of achievement: satisfying average calculable purposes whatever they may be. It has no connection with the kind of life that is free to discover or determine its own purposes. It therefore conflicts with Kantian morality in which, according to MacIntyre, "Weberian individualism" has its origins.

More generally, while utilitarianism is the precursor of bureaucratic rationalism, Kantianism is the precursor to the modern claims of individualism and "rights."[13] In the Kantian view, morality requires a self-sufficiency of meaning and value, which is the autonomous will of a rational agent. Its ancestry lies in the stoical tradition[14] according to which a rational being will regard virtue as its own end independent of

---

[11] Ibid., chs. 4 and 5.
[12] Ibid., p. 63.
[13] Ibid., p. 71.
[14] Ibid., p. 236.

conventions. The test of morality is whether one can will that the maxim of one's action be universalized. Its concern is with principles of abstract freedom, principles that recognize the capacity of the individual to determine his or her own purposes independent of the calculation of "morally neutral facts." Utilitarianism assumes that moral problems can be rationally solved by taking account of the interests of strategically motivated actors in light of their pre-moral purposes. Kantianism, however, assumes that strategic motivations leave us unfree to express ourselves rationally—since moral action, for a rational being, must consist in its own non-contingent motivation. Moral value is constituted only by considering humanity in ourselves and others as infinitely perfectible and not programmed for fulfilment by any conception of the "good" or any primary attachment to self-interest.

For MacIntyre the two apparently conflicting strands of modern morality have more commonalities than differences. If they seem to be different it is because utilitarianism grounds morality in morally neutral facts of human striving and the optimum rules for organizing it, while for Kantianism the ground of moral action is an independence from morally neutral facts such as our contingent socialization and considerations of prudence. The most obvious parallel, however, is that each approach regards morality from a universalistic standpoint, beyond tradition. The claims of justice appeal only to ideally rational individuals who need to possess no virtues, no competence in matters of justice, except for the capacity to decide for themselves the standards for judging the worthiness of their desires or the purpose of their lives.[15] The 'self' of modern morality is therefore conceived as having no constitutive features of identity, no relation to essential purposes against which the whole of one's life can be evaluated or in terms of which one's inclinations and desires can be poorly or well-shaped.[16]

According to MacIntyre, this stance of modern universalistic morality was adopted as an alternative to the older, predominantly Aristotelian, tradition of the "virtues." However, the defect of the modern approach is apparent from the virtues that are at least indirectly promoted in a liberal society, such as the capacity to function as a

---

[15] MacIntyre, *Whose Justice, Which Rationality?* p. 334.
[16] *After Virtue*, p. 204.

strategically effective role player or to define the value of selfhood apart from conventional role assignments or imposed values.[17]   At its most basic level the modern virtue is the capacity to separate one's self from one's role(s).[18]   By contrast the older conception of the virtues, in its ancient and medieval versions, implied a socially constituted self and institutions legitimately designed for the purpose of implementing values and conditioning the development of motives and intentions accordingly. In addition, moral value was considered intelligible only in the context of non-negotiable commitments to specific roles and activities that acquired their purpose in relation to a larger communal context.   It therefore expressed a relationship between one's personality and one's role that is neither socially contingent nor a matter of pure expediency.

MacIntyre is aware of the advantages liberals see in their anti-essentialist theory of human nature and their doctrine of public neutrality toward rival conceptions of the good.   The first is that a society founded on rational consent is possible only if individuals are freed from arbitrary power and authority.   The second is that the allegiance to the norms of justice need have no foundation other than enlightened self-interest or the capacity to tolerate significant levels of private disagreement. However, MacIntyre insists that, in reality, a liberal society must breed an emotivist culture.   The result is a simultaneous affirmation of arbitrary freedom and pure expedience which, according to MacIntyre, obliterates "the distinction between manipulative and non-manipulative social relationships."[19]

What an emotivist culture needs in order to conceal its flawed and incoherent moral foundations is a series of typical characters, figures in whom personality and role are fused, lending moral legitimacy to its "mode of social existence".[20]   There are therefore three authority figures that modern society has invented for this purpose: managers to control power and wealth, therapists to devise strategies for coping with conflicting roles and the burdens of choice, and rich aesthetes to serve as exemplars of convention-free self-expression.   In all three cases the

---

[17] Ibid., pp. 118, 205.
[18] Ibid., p. 220.
[19] Ibid., p. 25.
[20] Ibid., pp. 28–9.

tension between subjective morality and objective authority is safely removed. The meaning and function of the activities in which each kind of pseudo-objective authority excels can supposedly be established beyond the mere subjectivism of moral judgement. Consequently the fact that in each case authority has become nothing more than successful power is made unproblematic.[21]

MacIntyre therefore claims that the Weberian world can be made to appear relatively seamless in the areas of bureaucracy, therapy and aesthetic liberation. In these areas it does not matter that morality is based on subjective choice while non-moral considerations of efficiency govern our functional lives. Tensions and "disjunctions" between the spheres become neutralized. But in the political realm the basic moral incoherence is harder to conceal. Here, each approach, despite the putative rationality of its central claims, can justify only its usefulness for the respective social interests it is designed to serve.[22] MacIntyre suggests that Kantian claims to rights serve the function of "protest" whereas claims to utilitarian rationality serve the function of efficient implementation of goals established in advance. Furthermore, he insists that in a modern society someone's rights are always being invaded by someone else's interest in utility. This, of course, echoes Weber's observation about the ambivalence of justice after the breakdown of rational natural law. Weber argues that legal norms can be justified either in the name of substantive justice or—for those who have the resources to assert their power through the impartial mechanisms of bargaining and exchange—in the name of formal legality.[23]

For MacIntyre, however, the contrast of utilitarianism with the Kantian focus on rights and autonomy shows that, despite their incompatible premises, each of the theories trade equally in moral fictions. The standards according to which moral claims can be rationally justified are incompatible, since debate about which premises provide the best foundations for resolving the conflict is known to be interminable by each side. At several points Macintyre says that this accounts for the "shrillness" of moral debate in the modern public

---

[21] Ibid., p. 26.
[22] Ibid., pp. 70–1.
[23] *Economy and Society*, vol. 2, p. 886.

realm. MacIntyre concludes that there is no non-controversial way of defining the rationality of the principles that might inform public discussion in a liberal society. This does not follow only from the fact that what modern society has become contradicts its ideals, but from the fact that what it has become is a result of a decisive distortion of moral phenomena. This distortion became inevitable once people started to believe that rationally justifiable moral principles could be found even though "no disposition to care for justice as such will be first required in order to be rational."[24]

Ours is therefore a society in which some will worry about how the rules of the game arbitrarily deny them effective means to express their preferences, and others about how the rules of the game become arbitrary when they are seen as more than neutral means to implement their preferences. The result is that

> in a society in which preferences, whether in the market or in politics or in private life, are assigned the place which they have in a liberal order, power lies with those who are able to determine what the alternatives are to be between which choices will be available. The consumer, the voter, and the individual in general are accorded the right of expressing their preferences for one or more out of the alternatives which they are offered, but the range of possible alternatives is controlled by an elite, and how they are presented is also so controlled. The ruling elites within liberalism are thus bound to value highly competence in the persuasive presentation of alternatives, that is, in the cosmetic arts. So a certain kind of power is assigned a certain kind of authority.[25]

Nothing could serve as a better summary of Weber's description of what liberal democracy has become under the influence of bureaucracy.[26]

MacIntyre argues that thinkers like Weber and Nietzsche help us understand how the project of Enlightenment liberalism fails in its own terms. They have shown that only by appealing to non-rational sources of belief can one be successful in solving disputes about values[27] and

---

[24] *Whose Justice, Which Rationality?*, p. 342.

[25] Ibid., p. 345.

[26] *Economy and Society*, vol. 2, pp. 1396, 1449ff; Cf. Marcuse's contribution to *A Critique of Pure Tolerance* (with R.P. Wolff and B. Moore Jr.).

[27] *After Virtue*, p. 12.

that modern forms of authority can only justify their claims to the extent that they adopt the form of disguised power. According to MacIntyre, the fact that Weber did not admit to the latter point makes him complicit in the failure of Enlightenment culture, despite his otherwise portentous insights.[28] In either case the "Enlightenment project" was bound to fail and it was bound to look for substitutes for the conceptions of virtue at the center of the older, Aristotelian tradition. It was doomed, however, once it had rejected any natural telos of moral life itself. Modern culture had always been lying in wait for Nietzsche to explain all rational moral claims "in terms of a set of rationalizations which conceal the fundamentally non-rational phenomena of the will."[29] Contemporary liberals must therefore turn the rationally unresolvable conflict of values into a virtue itself. And there will always be thinkers like Nietzsche and Weber who can show that the idea that the liberal state can function as a truce-keeping institution is merely a fiction. As MacIntyre puts it : "Modern politics is civil war carried on by other means."[30]

MacIntyre's Alternative to Liberal Morality

According to MacIntyre, even liberalism cannot do without some theory of the good, some discrimination between more and less choiceworthy ways of life. Liberalism assumes that the objectivity of its rule-based conception of justice comes from the fact that rules and pure procedure apply only to those aspects of our social and political lives that are negotiable or to our access to the basic resources for expressing our preferences. The key point is the assumption that justice can be objective and impartial only when it does not reflect any agreed-upon system of values. MacIntyre argues that the moral self-confidence of modern society is sustained by the belief that moral issues in a pluralist society can be resolved only by a form of justice based on rationally determined rules[31] and impartial procedures for regulating conflict and competition.

---

[28] Ibid., p. 109.
[29] Ibid., p. 117.
[30] Ibid., p. 235.
[31] Ibid., p. 119.

This is why he enlists sociologists like Weber and Erving Goffman to help us understand the real nature of those features that define modern society as a flawed moral tradition. What is the resource for judging a tradition? It is a description of a society's specific moral tone and its more or less conscious way of producing certain types of character and sustaining itself, or undermining itself, by promoting certain kinds of virtue. In this regard MacIntyre proclaims that his argument against modern liberal individualism must be comparative and historicist. The standard for evaluating a moral tradition will be its coherence, or the particular relationship established in it between the meaning and use of its fundamental concepts. The Aristotelian tradition of the virtues that he wants to promote can only be rationally defended today as a rival to the competing tradition or traditions. The comparison must take the form of a "dramatic narrative," displaying the relative coherence and consistency of each tradition in its own terms and as a competitor with others. For its part, the modern tradition sees itself as an alternative to the older Aristotelian tradition and in fact views independence from tradition as the basis of its universal appeal.[32] But the point MacIntyre makes is not simply that the modern tradition fails in its own terms (which it does to the extent that the belief in its universal appeal masks an underlying moral confusion), but does so in a way that shows both how its own resources fail it and how the resources of the older tradition provide a more coherent fit between the meaning and use of moral concepts.

MacIntyre therefore attempts to equip the Aristotelian tradition with the means for rationally defending itself in a way that it never thought necessary. The first way he does this is by translating the teleological assumptions of Aristotelian morality into a form that will be a convincing alternative to modern conceptions of virtue. In the modern view there are no things or activities that are "good for" human beings, except with reference to the benefits to be derived from them, or the freedom or convenience they afford us in pursuing the good as we define it for ourselves. This leads to the separation between facts and values which was foreign to the older, Aristotelian-informed moral

---

[32] Ibid., p. 222.

traditions. Being anti-teleological, the modern tradition cannot derive what is 'good for' human beings from a rational understanding of their essential nature or basic needs. MacIntyre's claim is that we can still define what is good for human beings in a rational way without relying on Aristotle's "metaphysical biology" with its idea that the conditions for human fulfilment are programmed into us by nature. What we need to retain from Aristotle is the idea that "the virtues" are means to human fulfilment that are internally related to some objective standard by which the good life is defined. The concept of a virtue can be a source of ethical meaning only if the resources of one's moral tradition provide a way of defining intrinsic or internal standards of success in human affairs.[33] This, for example, is the function of the Greek conception of a polis. As members of a polis we see ourselves as part of a form of life in which not only the conditions of human fulfilment or individuality are secured—as in utilitarianism—but that success in that way of life is constitutively related to the evaluative standards provided by its model of admirable human achievement.[34]

MacIntyre fills out his conception of the virtues by connecting it to his much-discussed concept of "goods internal to a practice."[35] A practice is an activity requiring a specialized type of competence which is necessary for participating in it and for recognizing the achievements of those who excel in it. Achievement in a practice is met with disinterested appreciation of distinctive human qualities by its participants, and the competence involved can be judged, shared or further developed by those who can understand what are the internal goods involved in it. Therefore the human qualities involved cannot be confined to technical skill, but must be able to be developed in a more dynamic way. A practice is an area of life in which one must learn to appreciate excellence in others, be open to new standards of excellence and be capable of exemplifying them oneself. What makes chess, as opposed to tic-tac-toe, a practice is that the distinctive human qualities that are displayed must be taken seriously to judge and recognize its internal goods. Hence the pursuit of external goods such as money,

---

[33] Ibid., pp. 149, 184.
[34] *Whose Justice, Which Rationality?*, chs. 6, 7 and 8.
[35] Ibid., pp. 187ff.

power, status and 'entertainment value' cannot be the basis of the serious participation and the type of enjoyment that characterizes a practice.

But MacIntyre knows that almost any activity that is sufficiently complex and challenging and which has intrinsic appeal for serious participants may qualify as a practice. At the same time, he wants the notion of a 'practice' to define what is at least preparatory for a life of moral seriousness. He therefore lists "the virtues of justice, courage and honesty" as a necessary part of any practice. But these virtues, as Richard Bernstein has pointed out,[36] seem to make sense only in more general contexts. One cannot be a genuine specialist in justice, that is, in the way "merit" is to be recognized in a particular practice, without having an idea about how such judgement might apply to other practices and the relation between different kinds of practices. This is why Aristotle himself defined justice as the ultimate moral-political virtue. Moreover, MacIntyre says that one might have to be willing to risk personal security and comfort to excel in a practice. But in this connection even he concedes that achieving the internal goods connected with justice may actually be in conflict with achieving the internal goods of courage.[37] Finally his definition of practice does not entail that one must put internal goods before external goods in all of one's activities.

In light of such difficulties MacIntyre knows that a convincing moral teleology will require a more overarching conception of "the good of a human life conceived as a unity."[38] But even here, as many commentators have pointed out,[39] his account seems to undermine itself in its aim of achieving a contrast with modern moral concepts. He defines the good of a whole life as what gets embedded in a "narrative quest" or a life that can account for itself in terms of teleological "integrity and constancy."[40] Here MacIntyre is employing essential

---

[36] Richard Bernstein, "Nietzsche or Aristotle?: Reflections on Alasdaire MacIntyre's *After Virtue*", in his *Philosophical Profiles*, pp. 125–6.

[37] *After Virtue*, p. 200.

[38] Ibid., p. 203.

[39] In addition to Bernstein see also, Fred Dallmayr, "Virtue and Tradition" in his *Critical Encounters: Between Philosophy and Politics* and Charles Larmore, *Patterns of Moral Complexity*, ch. 2.

[40] *After Virtue*, p. 219.

elements of the Nietzschean and Weberian conception of personality, albeit with the hope of overcoming the loss of objective moral values that his modern rivals had portrayed. Nevertheless, it is hard for him to avoid re-stating the problem of moral objectivity in terms that are thoroughly consistent with the teleological indeterminacy of individual morality:

> the good life for man is the life spent in seeking for the good life for man, and the virtues necessary for the seeking are those which will enable us to understand what more and what else the good life for man is.[41]

Even when MacIntyre turns to the "concept of a tradition" to suggest that one cannot even think of one's life as essentially related to a meaningful tradition of moral argument except in certain kinds of well-formed historical and social contexts (like a polis) he has trouble providing a clear criterion that could rationally resolve the issue that divides the two traditions. Indeed the very criterion he sets up—that is, a tradition that works, or is open to being enhanced—is, by the terms of his own argument, a criterion in need of substantiation in terms of considerations about what kind of person one understands oneself to be.[42] MacIntyre never offers any objective criterion for making a decision in this regard, but he suggests that the ancient tragedians (as opposed to modern decisionists like Weber), knew that the tragic quality of the choice did not lessen the objective claims of the competing ends. Unfortunately MacIntyre does not linger long enough on this theme to see that Weber himself had wanted to recover this same sense of tragedy that could manifest itself in morally serious action.[43] Instead MacIntyre

---

[41] Ibid.

[42] *Whose Justice, Which Rationality?*, p. 394.

[43] It is implausible to identify Weber's position in an unqualified way with that of emotivism (Habermas, *Moral Consciousness and Communicative Action*, p. 187), but to the extent that he does MacIntyre makes the following observation: "...the Sophoclean self differs from the emotivist self as much as does the heroic self, although in more complex ways. The Sophoclean self transcends the limitations of social roles and is able to put those roles in question, but it remains accountable to the point of death and accountable precisely for the way it handles itself in those conflicts which make the heroic point of view no longer possible. Thus the presupposition of the Sophoclean self's existence is that it can indeed win or lose,

says that the virtue which must support the rational ordering of moral virtues and the pursuit of internal goods is the "virtue of having an adequate sense of the traditions to which one belongs or which confront one." One therefore needs to be part of a "living tradition" to have "an adequate sense of tradtion [which] manifests itself in a grasp of those future possibilities which the past has made available to the present."[44]

In MacIntyre's account, the goals of freedom and rationality that remained so ambiguous and challenging for Weber are deprived of meaning by the emptiness of the social life within which contemporary moral argument must live and breathe. The Nietzschean view of "the great man", or Weber's rarification of moral seriousness and genuine politics, appear to MacIntyre as the logical culmination of a tradition lacking the resources of a vital moral tradition. It is therefore no accident to him that these conceptions can be used to cut short moral discussion. By denying, as liberalism has, the rootedness of moral personality in systems of shared values, one can only see Nietzschean individualism as a vice turned into a virtue. MacIntyre therefore concludes that we can only really overcome the fatal mistakes of the modern project by turning away from the anti-communitarianism of Nietzsche and Weber toward the "moral particularity" of local communities resistant to bureaucratic individualism.[45]

But has MacIntyre really made progress beyond Weber and Nietzsche? As an attempt to define the possibility of rationally arriving at objective moral standards, MacIntyre's books clearly presuppose what needs to be demonstrated, namely, that rationality can be possible only in a tradition whose resources for addressing moral problems allow it to work better at identifying genuine attempts to solve those problems. In this case the "resource" is pre-defined as a shared value-standpoint, and the test of whether it works is its ability to survive serious encounters with other traditions that take morality equally seriously.[46] The modern

---

save itself or go to moral destruction, that there is an order which requires from us the pursuit of certain ends, an order relationship to which provides our judgements with the property of truth or falsity." (*After Virtue*, pp. 143–5).

[44] Ibid., p. 223.

[45] Ibid., p. 263.

[46] *Whose Justice, Which Rationality?*, pp. 397ff.

tradition, by contrast, has as its only resource the denial that important moral questions have objective answers. It comes to the enterprise of moral theory with the idea that truth claims made within moral traditions are based on arbitrary presuppositions, and that the truths themselves can only be defended as useful beliefs. It turns out that once MacIntyre gets liberalism to think of itself as a "tradition" he can play a clever game of 'loser wins'. The liberal tradition spawns a relativist moral epistemology which states that the success of a tradition can only be defined in its own terms, and that these terms are not themselves subject to rational debate. Its relativists and perspectivists assert the rationally irresolvable nature of moral conflicts in order to serve their own tradition's arbitrary aim, that of disqualifying (as morally incompetent) from its discussions on morality those who think the point of such discussions is to discover objective moral truths.

We will have occasion to look at a somewhat similar argument made in a different context by Leo Strauss. For now, however, it is important to examine more closely whether MacIntyre has provided a fair portrait of the characteristics of liberalism in his account of its moral bankruptcy.

SAVING LIBERALISM FROM ITS VICES

In the first place we can note that one of the leading contemporary liberal philosophers, John Rawls, has tried to refashion his defence of liberalism to meet some of the objections of communitarian thinkers like MacIntyre. In his later writings Rawls contends that the advantage of liberal democratic justice is that it is grounded neither in metaphysical conceptions of selfhood or autonomy, nor in a philosophical position that implies moral scepticism. Rather its starting point requires only that, for the purposes of resolving questions of justice and mutually advantageous cooperation, we presuppose a "desire for free and uncoerced agreement."[47] He insists that "justice as fairness" can provide a morally justified conception of political life without trying to resolve any debate regarding the objectivity of moral standards. In this sense one of the tests of a good social and political order must be that it

---

[47] John Rawls, "Justice as Fairness: Political, not Metaphysical," p. 223.

will not be structured so as to dispose people to enter political discussions for the sake of pressing their views on philosophically controversial topics such as the nature of the good life. This is because liberal justice only needs to be sustained by an "overlapping consensus," which does not have to be seen as anything more than a result of our society's historically specific commitment to overcome the undesirable effects of controversy about the good.[48]

However, Rawls' liberalism appears to MacIntyre as a pragmatic necessity arbitrarily defined as a moral achievement. This is why those like Richard Rorty and Jeffrey Stout, who want to defend some version of Rawlsian liberalism, have tried to devise a better response to MacIntyre. That is, they do not ask whether liberalism is based on the right way of understanding a moral achievement, but on what desirable things follow from "our" particular, historically contingent understanding of justice that would make us want to identify with it as a moral achievement appropriate for a society like ours.

Rawls himself does not try to neutralize claims about the unavoidable moral skepticism of liberalism in this manner. He argues that, from the standpoint of liberal values, philosophical controversies are too deep and important to be settled in political terms.[49] But he later on admits that the theorist of liberal justice cannot be indifferent to how the outcome of the philosophical debate of the theory (especially regarding the success of charges of moral scepticism) itself might condition its acceptance.[50] In effect, Rawls concedes that MacIntyre's suspicions may turn out to be justified: in order for Rawlsian liberalism to qualify as a morally serious way of life it must screen out—because of their possible social and political impact—many of the questions philosophers must eventually take seriously.

I will return to this question in my discussion of Strauss below. For now, however, it is useful to look at how MacIntyre's account of practices can be used to evaluate the dilemmas of liberal justice in light

---

[48] For a recent defense of Rawls' construct of an overlapping consensus which takes account of the objections of MacIntyre see Jeffrey Stout, *Ethics After Babel: On the Languages of Morals and their Discontents*, pp. 213, 225-7.

[49] "Justice as Fairness: Political, not Metaphysical," p. 230.

[50] Ibid., p. 250.

of his assumptions about the nature of liberal institutions. In the midst of his discussion MacIntyre proposes firstly, that all practices, the pursuit of internal goods, cannot be totally independent of the pursuit of external goods, and, secondly, that institutions are required for this latter activity:

> institutions and practices characteristically form a single causal order in which the ideals and the creativity of the practice are always vulnerable to the acquisitiveness of the institution in which the cooperative care for common goods of the practice is always vulnerable to the competitiveness of the institution. In this context the essential function of the virtues is clear. Without them, without justice, courage and truthfulness, practices could not resist the corrupting power of institutions.[51]

MacIntyre's next few pages resemble some aspects of Weber's analysis of the crowding out of value rationality by instrumental rationality under modern conditions. But he suggests that for any society it is the function of the virtues to present a "potential stumbling block to...comfortable ambition."[52] Here MacIntyre is involved in a reflection on the problem of 'substantive irrationality' as an endemic possibility facing institutions and their regulation. Moreover, substantive irrationality seems inevitable in modern society, as MacIntyre understands it, since any consensus or rational discussion of values can only be a temporary truce in a larger context in which someone's strategic interests must triumph over those of someone else.

But it is important to recognize that some liberal social theorists have argued, in a post-Weberian vein, that pluralist liberal democracies are actually enhanced by formally rational institutions. Weber had proposed that in a modern system of rational-legal authority only bureaucratic institutions can fulfil the demands of democratization. Hence an institution like a political party must be specialized to convert its effectiveness into a resource like power. In MacIntyre's terms, in order to be effective, citizens and elites must play by the rules of organized power, with the result that "internal goods" must be pursued in a competitive context governed largely by the acquisition of "external

---

[51] *After Virtue*, p. 194.
[52] Ibid., p. 194.

goods." In this sense the modern state's adherence to liberal democratic norms, and therefore its legitimacy, can only be nominal. However it is notable that many contemporary liberals believe that this result of bureaucratic organization does not have the "substantively irrational" consequences that either MacIntyre or Weber thinks it does.

In Parsons' view, in a complex liberal society even a resource like power, which allows a fluid mobilization of "commitments or obligation for effective collective action,"[53] can be regulated in terms that affirm or stabilize the larger normative culture. In any complex society power and money are necessary as fluid resources that, in order to be adaptable to the interests of strategic actors, must function independently of contextual considerations. MacIntyre showed how authority and recognition naturally gravitate to those who are qualified to achieve the non-neutral, context-sensitive goods involved in practices. Parsons wants to show how generalized media like power and money also have a legitimate use. In order to ensure "flexible, market-like" exchanges between the state and the voters, or between firms and households, these media must be sufficiently context-independent. However, modernization, or social differentiation, does not promote alienation simply because families and citizens no longer have direct, intimate contact with many of the "real" goods which are the input and output of the institutions themselves.[54] Rather, the gains in flexibility outweigh the losses. This is because modern society has created new kinds of authorities (professionals rather than bureaucrats) who, in principle, know how, and are constrained, to use generalized resources wisely—in the form of tax revenues, electoral support and accumulated capital.

According to Parsons the normative culture of a liberal society can ultimately be successfully institutionalized only in the form of trust. Because we live in a complex society we need to delegate authority for the sake of efficiency and for the sake of making freedom of choice and justice effective. Therefore the justice of the system (its "substantive

---

[53] Talcott Parsons, *Politics and Social Structure*, p. 382.

[54] See Leon Mayhew's excellent summaries of Parsons' theory of generalized media as a re-statement of the liberal theory of institutions in his introduction to Talcott Parsons, *On Institutions and Social Evolution*, ed., Mayhew, and his "In Defense of Modernity: Talcott Parsons and the Utilitarian Tradition," pp. 1273–1305.

rationality") can in a sense be grounded only in the trust that rides relatively freely upon the system's formal effectiveness. This is the only way of organizing the normative culture of a complex society, where, in effect, every participant must live with contextually neutral political procedures and economic demands that accumulate deposits of trust in organizations that reinforce specialization and calculability (bureaucracy and work). For Parsons this does not lead to a social pattern in which goods like power and money must take precedence over internal goods, nor does it lead to bureaucratic or elite expropriation of politics by means of formally liberal institutions. Rather, the concentration of money and power is best seen as a case of loaning a generalizable resource which may in fact put the creditor in an even better position to optimize her access to the non-generalizable goods to be found in contextually sensitive areas of personal self-realization (family, community, occupational achievement).

Parsons thinks of liberal politics as analogous to a banking system where the public are shareholders or depositors, civil servants are operational staff and leaders are entrepreneurial trustees focusing on long term strategy.[55] In this sense, members of the public exercise power through elections by depositing it in institutions specialized in responsibly and effectively managing it. This allows a generalizable and benign increase in the productivity of power so long as neither the public, the bureaucrats nor the leaders try to realize, for its own sake, the cash value of their lent or borrowed power. Increases in the productivity of power mitigate the zero-sum effects of power relation-ships, making it more possible to derive income, context-sensitive services and a larger pool of power-funds to invest in the future. Power will itself be poorly invested when it is utilized solely for the purposes of hierarchical control just as money is poorly invested when it is used as a means of comfortable ambition. Systems of power, however, cannot give every legal owner of the resource the right to participate directly in decisions affecting her interests. Formally rational institutions, such as legal-rational authority, can therefore be seen as inherently risky instruments of liberal democracy which, nevertheless,

---

[55] Parsons, *Politics and Social Structure*, pp. 392–4.

allow more adaptable and flexible expression of the goals for the sake of which we cooperate, such as democracy and solidarity.[56]

Parsons and Weber agree that if organized power is to be harnessed to "normative culture" its claims cannot be exclusively concerned with success or with the direct expression of ideal goals (such as perfectly rational and informed consent). But for Weber this meant that power must prove itself as responsibility for shaping, and courageously confronting, the future of conflict and struggle in one's society. This is because power cannot effectively legitimize itself by employing the sanctions it holds in reserve, and must thereby cultivate belief in the validity of its claim to authority by more or less symbolic means. By the same token, however, Weber had trouble distinguishing legitimate authority from successful power. For Parsons, by contrast, power proves itself by its social productivity and its capacity to be creatively expanded, thereby contingently allowing normative culture or solidarity to be sustained and improved in unexpected ways.[57]

But even here Parsons needs another "medium" besides money and power. Hence he develops his notion of the "influence" medium which, unlike that of power, refers to the mobilization of loyalties:

> In the field of influence, the analogy with banking and credit seems most obvious in connection with the allocation of loyalties. The postulate on which our whole analysis in this area is based is that it applies most clearly to a highly pluralistic social system in which the allocation of loyalties cannot be wholly based on direct assessment of the importance of the intrinsic issues involved, but that commitments are widely made in response to influence...My suggestion is that the principal way in which this is done in a society like the American is through voluntary associations...[S]uch an association often does more than simply collect increments of influence; it creates the effect of adding to the total amount of influence in circulation.[58]

Parsons goes on to speak of the room for "independent judgement" this gives to such "influence bankers." Here he is thinking of the capacity

---

[56] Mayhew, "In Defense of Modernity," p. 1298ff.

[57] Parsons, "On the Concept of Influence," in *On Institutions and Social Evolution*, ed., Mayhew, p. 250.

[58] Ibid., p. 251.

to make investments in preparing for the future, which is threatened in a society which distrusts the short-run unaccountability of professional elites, university professors and the like. Nevertheless he admits that there is a "fine line between solid, responsible and constructive leadership...and reckless overextendedness."[59]

What Parsons' conception of vetical trust lacks is highlighted by more nuanced ideas such as that of "complex equality" elaborated by Michael Walzer. Parsons wants to defend a conception of "non-ascriptive" inequality or meritocracy. He claims that this exemplifies modern society's need for a "functional equivalent of aristocracy" which he suggests has been undermined by indiscriminately overextending egalitarian prerogatives into areas where they do not belong, namely, in the society's prestige system.[60] It is characteristic of Parsons to attribute problems like indiscriminate equality and resentment of meritocratic power to the growing pains of modernization, rather than to some fairly obvious problems associated with consumer capitalism and the "entrepreneurialization" of professions like law and medicine. Here we do better by following Walzer who argues that discriminating equality can be an intelligible part of liberal justice only if justice is also like practical wisdom. Liberalism is not incompatible with Aristotelian practical wisdom so long as context-sensitivity within a given sphere of practice is not undermined by authority and control acquired on the basis of considerations external to that sphere. This is often the threat when large claims are made in favor of competence in the management of context-independent goods like money, power and influence (prestige).[61]

But in our context we must note the differences between Parsons' and Weber's understanding of organized power and influence. For Parsons influence is utilized (well or poorly) by the way a leader assumes the right to speak in an independently persuasive way for others rather than by the way an "official" effectively manages a formal

---

[59] *Politics and Social Structure*, p. 391.

[60] Parsons, "Equality and Inequality in Modern Society," in *his Social Systems and the Evolution of Action Theory*, p. 348, 354, 363.

[61] See generally, Walzer, *Spheres of Justice: A Defense of Pluralism and Equality.*

mandate or right to use coercion as an inducement.[62]   Influence therefore supplements power without necessarily being reducible to it as Weber thought.[63] This is because power is ultimately backed by the material means of conditioning the alternatives of others, while influence, or generalized persuasiveness, is backed by the capacity to appeal to materially unsanctionable commitments such as beliefs and ideal goals. Weber, as we have seen, saw these two different ways of mobilizing support as just two different aspects of power, the latter simply being more effective. But for Parsons legitimate authority is not based solely on voluntary compliance with the strategic goals of organized interests, but on the capacity of disinterested trustees to manage long-term deposits of loyalty so that everyone's chances of achieving their internal, context-sensitive goods may be enhanced in the long run.

Jürgen Habermas has noted the importance of Parsons's subtle analysis. But he has rightly made criticisms that remind us of MacIntyre's scepticism about the fate of "practices" and the capacity to sustain "virtues" in modern society as it is presently organized. He argues that Parsons' influence medium (as well as his "value commitments" medium) assumes that policy justifications and moral arguments are capable of being treated as augmentable resources of strategic action and as the functional equivalent to more direct appeal to the realm of shared cultural traditions, internal goods and "mutual understanding."[64] Parsons does not see that the normative culture of a society is distorted when the "life-world" or the realm of practices gets operationalized in this way, that is, "when we make manipulative use of non-manipulable goods."[65] By contrast, Habermas appreciates Weber's and Marx's sensitivity to the way in which bureaucratic capitalism has alienated the autonomy of citizens, workers, families and educational institutions by over-extending the use of power and money as action-coordinating media. He insists that if influence and value commitments are used in the same way one is assuming that consensual action and the

---

[62] Parsons, "On the Concept of Influence," p. 239-38.
[63] *Politics and Social Structure*, p. 388, 394.
[64] Jürgen Habermas, *The Theory of Communicative Action*, vol. 2, p. 275.
[65] Ibid., pp. 275, 267, 277.

achievement of internal goods can only be made more rational through strategic action. Parsons has merely taken over Weber's understanding of the irresistibility of bureaucracy, while subtracting the latter's insight into its culturally stultifying effects.

Habermas has shown that Parsons' formulations really only beg the questions raised by Weber's diagnosis of the paradoxical development of modernity; he suggests that normatively unregulated trust in the responsibility of leaders and experts is defined in an *a priori* way as the basis of new freedoms and a more creative form of moral solidarity.[66] In a diametrically opposed manner, MacIntyre proposes we can break free of the moral paradoxes of Weberian modernity only by recovering a sense of the superiority of pre-modern moral traditions. As we shall see in the next chapter, Habermas' work takes a middle path, one that tries to reconstruct the achievements of modern society in a way that does not assume that liberal-democratic institutions must undermine the ideals they were set up to serve.

---

[66] Ibid., pp. 291–92.

Chapter Four

THE MODERNIZATION OF POLITICAL REASON: REFLECTIONS ON HABERMAS

In the previous chapters I have explored some of the political consequences of 'disenchantment' in Weber and the work of later theorists. I have connected Weber's analyses of the tension between democracy and bureaucracy to other diagnoses of modern political culture which try to fault Weber for either overgeneralizing this tension or failing to draw the right conclusions about the moral tradition from which it stems. It is the merit of Habermas' work that he does not fall prey either to Parsons' overly "harmonious" picture of modern "institutionalized individualism," or to the *tout court* rejection of modern value-pluralism on the grounds that the latter cannot be moral and prudent at the same time. In this chapter we cannot discuss the full compass of Habermas' detailed and elaborate response to Max Weber's thought. My focus will therefore be directed at two crucial and interrelated themes—first, Habermas' critique of Weber's theory of legitimacy and, second, the shortcomings he finds in Weber's account of the limits of rationality in social theory and political action.

THE SOCIOLOGY OF MODERN POLITICS
AFTER WEBER

We have seen that for Weber the legitimacy of legal power is based on the belief that the enacted order is procedurally correct and that obedience is owed to impersonal, abstract rules. But the corresponding effect of rationalization occurs only to the extent that actors and organized interests can thereby expect decisions to be regulated, not by principles of substantive justice or "consideration," but by conditions which make possible the peaceful, rule-bound adjudication of conflicts.[1] Weber insists that the indirect consequence of the Rights of Man— especially the ideals of "formal legal equality"—was to facilitate the procedural rationality that dominates modern life, and which is the source of legitimation of positive law.[2] As a result, confidence in the function of the formal rationalization of the legal system has become more important for its legitimacy than the moral grounding of the consensual order intended by the rights and freedoms in the name of which it had been established.

In this respect both Habermas and Wolfgang Schluchter have argued that Weber held a one-sided view of the developmental significance of modern law. Weber assumed that the rationalization of law must be sacrificed to a kind of ideological dogfight whenever considerations of substantive justice are introduced as the basis of the legitimacy of the legal system itself.[3] According to Habermas the key problem here is that Weber had to rely upon a "decisionististic concept of legitimacy through procedure" which is based upon a selective outcome of the process of rationalization of modern legal-administrative systems: by detaching itself from moral-practical legitimizing grounds, modern law becomes "an instrument for realizing any values and interests whatever."[4]

Habermas claims that Weber's concept of "belief in legality," like that of Parsons' legitimation by trust, merely empirically takes for granted the outcome of consensus formation that it needs to be effective in producing legitimacy. Even in the case of "legitimation by procedure"—in which legitimacy is based on an empirically effective acceptance of the functional authority of rational problem-solvers—the belief in validity of the impersonal order is based on the implicit

---

[1] *Economy and Society*, vol. 2, p. 811; Cf. Wolfgang Schluchter, *The Rise of Western Rationalism*, pp. 108-9.

[2] *Economy and Society*, vol. 2, p. 1209.

[3] Ibid., p. 866ff; Habermas, *The Theory of Communicative Action*, vol 1, pp. 266–270; Schluchter, *The Rise of Western Rationalism*, pp. 116ff.

[4] Habermas, *Theory of Communicative Action*, vol 1, pp. 264, 262.

assumption that qualified persons can give "good reasons" for the existence of some rule or the interpretation of the problems being addressed.[5] Habermas proposes that modern legal rationalization does indeed extend the distance between law and morality. However its institutions can never become legitimate by separating the positive legal order from the expectation that the requirement of justifying it in a principled way (rather than simply cultivating voluntary support) could be satisfied.

Habermas does not contest Weber's assertion that legitimacy claims in the modern world must come up against the conflict of ultimate values. But he does not thereby accept Weber's assumption that the acceptance of legitimacy claims can be based merely on a sufficiency of empirical acceptance. This is because empirical acceptance cannot be distinguished from an effect of power that is in need of legitimation. Rather Habermas argues that legitimacy claims can be rationally grounded even if they are not taken as expressions of claims about the validity of values or as the result of a consensus informed by a true account of the world or common interests. He argues that not every attempt to understand legitimacy in terms of justice must come down to competing faiths or "ultimate grounds."[6] Whenever it is necessary to evaluate independently the potential reasons underlying a legitimacy claim then the very conception of an effective agreement can no longer be empirical—rather it presupposes the possibility of taking a position on its "claim to motivate rationally."[7]

It is precisely whenever motives and reasons have to be connected in this way—that is, in terms of possible discursive participation—that it is possible to speak of the "truth-dependency" of legitimacy claims.[8] This claim to motivate rationally is only effective in the context of "practical discourse" which is a procedural ideal from which modern justice receives its normative content. Although modern institutions rarely actualize this ideal, it is presupposed by the very concept of legitimacy under which they operate: "Only the rules and

---

[5] Ibid., p. 265, 267.

[6] Habermas, *Communication and the Evolution of Society*, p. 200.

[7] Habermas, *Legitimation Crisis*, p. 97–8.

[8] Ibid.

communicative presuppositions that make it possible to distinguish an accord or agreement among free and equals from a contingent or forced consensus have legitimating force today."[9]   According to Habermas, the normative force underlying the ideal of a communicatively achieved agreement cannot be dismissed simply by the fact that acceptance is often achieved empirically. This is because any attempt by organized power or a system of domination to rely solely on empirical acceptance circumvents, rather than replaces, the moral demand that social and political arrangements *not* be sustained on the basis of immunizing them from public scrutiny regarding what they do and the actual interests they express.

    We can compare Habermas' criticism of Weber with that of Niklas Luhmann. Luhmann, like Parsons, says that Weber wanted to define organizational rationality in terms of the older idea of the legitimation of authority, while at the same time realizing that rationality must selectively take account of the complex institutional preconditions of effective action. Hence Weber arrived at an only partially successful conception:

> A person who exercises domination has the opportunity to make his ends the ends of others. In addition, thanks to this opportunity he can devise new ends that he could never have fulfilled alone. Rationality is augmented to the extent that in general, he is in a position to dictate to others the premises for their decisions. As a consequence, the extent to which a social system becomes rationalized depends upon the basis and limits of this total acceptance.[10]

Luhmann goes on to argue that Weber could only vaguely point the way to a 'systems' conception of organizational rationality which would not rely on participatory consensus or the idea that social relationships require the whole person to be motivationally involved in them.[11] Luhmann's theory is much like Parsons' in that he thinks of rationality as a property of a "system" that has established freedom from concrete motivational contexts and has expanded "its temporal horizon ... for

---

[9] Habermas, *Communication and the Evolution of Society*, p. 188.
[10] Niklas Luhmann, *The Differentiation of Society*, p. 23.
[11] Ibid., p. 42.

planning and action."[12] The legitimacy of a system of positive law is therefore self-referential, and even self-created, since it is not based on value premises or even on empirical acceptance but on the "assumption of acceptance."[13] There is no procedural ideal from which law can be said to acquire its normative force since, for Luhmann, procedures are merely the way the system programs itself to respond to its environment. Truth and morality must be excluded from the legal system because law is "contingent"—it is both justified and created by decisions.[14]

As we have seen, Habermas believes that democratic legitimacy now presupposes a reference to a discursive procedural ideal with normative content. Weberian scepticism toward "ultimate grounds" does not imply scepticism toward morality altogether, but rather the potential for a more advanced, post-conventional stage of moral-practical consciousness. Habermas is therefore also opposed to Luhmann's "metabiological" conception of the human situation, with its assumption that learning and problem-solving is merely a process by which a system adapts to given or anticipated distinctions between itself and its environments.[15] Habermas argues that systems theory replaces the critical understanding of the way individuals and social classes become subject to the imperatives of domination by representing the same phenomena as a gain in the flexibility of society afforded by increasingly opening the definition of social issues to technical control and adaptation to self-referential procedure. Rationality must therefore be reduced to whatever allows a system to plan social change and adapt to the complexity of its environment.

From Habermas' standpoint this simply lends credence to Weber's pessimism about the fate of liberal democratic ideals since the forms of public rationality they require have been undercut by a purely nominal concern with 'substantive' goals such as universal freedoms, rights, inclusiveness and progress. Public rationality is absorbed by techno-

---

[12] Ibid., p. 43.

[13] Luhmann, *A Sociological Theory of Law*, p. 200–206.

[14] Ibid., p. 147–158.

[15] Habermas, "On Luhmann's Systems Theory of Society," in *Philosophical Discourse of Modernity*, pp. 368ff.

cratic or functional rationality and the dimension of moral-practical problems appears to become ever more subordinate to the question of whether the system is effectively programmed, flexible, and complex enough to sustain the requisite 'learning' processes in modern conditions of social differentiation. Habermas worries that system theorists have simply smoothed over the process by which democracy has been reduced to acclamation and liberal politics reduced to the most formally effective arrangement for processing strategically conditioned social choices. In the process public institutions are hijacked by the technocratic system itself through the dominance of the 'steering' media of power and money, as well as by the rule of experts and the organized leadership of public opinion.

By rejecting systems theory Habermas has taken aim at Weber's ambiguous and usually pessimistic conclusions about modern politics by fundamentally re-examining the 'decisionist' view of moral-practical life that Weber shares with Luhmann. He regrets that Weber's separation of truth from moral-practical problems left him with instrumental rationality as the "only aspect under which action can be criticized and improved." Habermas interprets the paradoxical development of modern rationalization as a selective distortion and narrowing of the possible meaning and scope of rationality in human affairs. He therefore wants to propose a recognition of the unrealized possibilities of ethical rationalism against Weber's interpretation of the fate of ethical meaning in Western culture. It will be important now to discuss this in the context of Weber's own account of the limits of rationality in science and politics.

THE CONSEQUENCES OF DISENCHANTMENT IN SCIENCE AND POLITICS

It has been said that Weber's 'philosophy' of social science moves haltingly between the two poles of practical irrationalism and cognitive rationalism.[16] Indeed Weber's basic view of scientific rationality and its

---

[16] This terminology is suggested in Phillipe Raynaud, *Max Weber et les dilemmes de la raison moderne*; Cf. Karl-Otto Apel, "The *a priori* of the Communication Community and The Foundations of Ethics," in *Toward a Transformation of*

relation to practical and evaluative questions is quite emblematic of his thought as a whole. Although on the one hand Weber sees discussions of values as meaningful, he insists they can only be subjected to "scientific criticism" as far as their "means" are concerned. The success of such investigations often depends on whether or not they inform the discussions of individuals and groups who share certain values or who are equally convinced of their validity. Only if they take place among adherents of competing values can such discussions serve to deepen the understanding of one's own value position.[17] Weber's position then seems to be that the connection between scientific reason and the problems of value judgements posed by practical situations is infused with contingency.

One of the consequences of disenchantment is therefore the idea that the power of scientific explanations of behaviour or historical phenomena does not extend as far as telling one how to choose among ultimate values. Of course if such choices are not capable of being rationally grounded it does not follow that they are devoid of any relation to objective value. Rather, Weber seems to lean upon a notion that he has in common with existentialism—that individuals create objective value through their "ultimate attitude toward life," and therefore by the meaning they give to the world through the force of their commitment. Portis notes that this idea is at the root of Weber's own attempt to overcome the fact-value distinction, which is said by many to be the most problematic aspect of his work:

> Whether value statements can be derived from fact statements is perhaps an interesting puzzle. It is relevant to social science, however, only if it is concluded that cognitive beliefs cannot logically require normative commitments. If identity is derived from cognitive beliefs, then cognitive beliefs do logically entail normative commitments. For self conception is a prerequisite for evaluation and choice, and the individual has no choice but to be committed to his or her self-concept. This self-concept cannot itself be a matter of choice. Consequently, its components are valued because they are incorporated into self-conception, not incorporated into self-conception because they are valued.[18]

Philosophy, p. 236ff.

[17] "The Meaning of Ethical Neutrality," p. 12.

[18] Portis, *Max Weber and Political Commitment: Science, Politics and Personality*,

If Portis is right, the basis of any concern with 'meaning' would then be the effort of an individual to become a personality, which is the only way a unity of subjectivity and objective value can be achieved. Of course this in no way resolves the difficulties associated with Weber's conception of socially indeterminate freedom to which I alluded above.

If one grants Weber this special interest of his science, there still remains his controversial claim that the study of meaningful behaviour can satisfy the criteria of epistemological rationality. Weber believed that his ideal type method could be used to achieve a "rational understanding" of the purposes toward which individual behaviour has been directed, but it can do so only in so far as it restricts itself to comparing the course of empirical events with a pragmatically selected normative criterion which he called the "objectively correct type."[19] In other words, as we mentioned above, Weber's methodology of interpretive science forbids treating ideal types as valid conclusions or causal inferences. This stems from his contention that empirical reality is itself meaningless from the standpoint of the purely causal investigation of empirical regularities.

Yet he supposed that, in the scientific investigation of meaningful phenomena, it is still possible to proceed from the assumption that causal explanation has legitimate analytical applicability. This is because instrumentally rational action allows one to assess the implications of an actor's own understanding of his or her situation in universalistic terms. Here the action situation is constructed so as to treat values only according to their influence upon the end to be sought, and therefore independently of the question of their validity. This allows one to assume that what "will usually be a most decisive causal factor for the external course— i.e. the 'outcome' of the action" is the degree to which the "value positions" of the actors lead them to deviate or conform to the "objectively correct type." Weber considered it essential for the scientist to realize that one can only treat the normative criteria one applies to the actions of others hypothetically, since in actual situations there is an infinite variety of possible interpretations of practical imperatives. Instrumentally rational action is only "the most

---

p. 110.
[19] Weber, "Some Categories of Interpretive Sociology," pp. 154–55.

understandable" kind of action in the sense that it is based on "judgements of average probable behaviour". But only the heuristic use of this type of action allows the observer to arrive at valid interpretations of the consistency of the action with the actor's effective context and subjective beliefs.[20]

But Weber is emphatic that science informs the actual search for solutions to practical problems as well as the conscious calculation of the reliability of means and probable outcomes. Indeed, in this respect there is an important distinction between 'rational understanding' and what he calls the 'objectivity of knowledge'. It is well known that Weber wants to unequivocally distinguish objectivity from an "attitude of moral indifference,"[21] a point that is often lost on critics who want to ascribe a positivist understanding of objectivity to him. Weber actually suggests that by 'objectivity' one is referring to a unique demand that derives from the scientist's understanding of the ultimate meaning of her conduct in her profession. It has been widely recognized that, for Weber, this demand for self-understanding appears also to demand that the scientist preserve a certain degree of independence from both the sphere of technical problem-solving (where the findings of science are obviously utilized) as well as from the sphere of the "acting, willing person."[22] If Weber is charged with being a positivist it is because he seems to support the idea that the significance of a valid scientific insight lies in its possible technical application and is therefore indifferent to the choice of practical premises which shapes substantive commitments in social and political affairs. From the standpoint of positivism, the goals of science stand outside the affirmation of, or compromises among, substantive aims which are a matter of contingent subjective decisions about ends.

---

[20] "Objectivity," p. 98; "Categories," p. 154; "Objectivity," p. 95; "Categories," p. 161; "Objectivity," p. 84.

[21] "The Meaning of Ethical Neutrality," p. 60.

[22] "Objectivity," p. 53; The surrounding passage is obviously one which justifies Ernst Troeltsch's characterization of Weber's thought as a "science-free position toward values" [*wissenschaftsfreie Wertposition*], an obvious twist on the notion of the value-freedom or value neutrality of science. See Troeltsch, *Der Historismus und seine Probleme*, in *Gesammelte Schriften*, Tübingen, 1922, p. 573, quoted in Eugen Fleischmann, "De Weber à Nietzsche," p. 225.

Hence the "obverse" of positivism is a kind of decisionism.[23] In this view the competence of science goes no further than monitoring the choice of means or informing decision-makers about the possible consequences of the attempt to realize their ends. As we have seen Habermas believes that the orientation to technical control privileged by positivism and the fact-value distinction has been a leading cause of the social and political discontents of modernity.

It is indeed difficult to avoid the conclusion that Weber's maxim of value-neutrality entails that science be marked off from the sphere of political commitment. For Weber, science makes us aware of the point at which a practical problem presents itself as a choice among competing values. Moreover it is precisely at this point, Weber argued, that arriving at compelling proofs or establishing facts will not suffice to equip either our action or our will with a better capacity to prove itself in the "struggle against the difficulties which life presents."[24] However, in recognition of this delimitation, Weber says that science plays a role "in the service of moral forces"—which means that its function is to instill in its addressees the desire to undertake acts of clarification and to gain the fullest possible knowledge of the implications of holding the values they do. Hence, beyond providing ways of calculating the probable consequences of possible actions (so that choices and deliberations may be more fully informed), science can help the acting, willing individual confront the "necessity of choice," help show her that ultimate values can often only be realized at the expense of one another, and urge her to better "think in terms of the context and meaning of the ends he desires and among which he chooses."[25] As we shall see, Schluchter believes there is promise in Weber's idea of "self control vis-a-vis one's own and alien 'gods'," an idea which avoids the twin dangers of technocratic science, which is 'world-mastery' without moral reflection and the contingency of pure, irrational commitment characteristic of decisionism.[26]

---

[23] Stephen P. Turner and Regis A. Factor, *Max Weber and the Dispute over Reason and Value*, pp. 217–18.

[24] "Objectivity," p. 55; See also Portis, *Max Weber and Political Commitment*, p. 81.

[25] "Science as a Vocation," p. 152; *On Universities*, p. 21; "Objectivity," p. 53.

[26] Schluchter, "The Paradox of Rationalization," in *Max Weber's Vision of History:*

Of course it is not even clear whether Weber's rationalistic understanding of science's own delimited role can be sustained under his all-important conception of "value relevance" in research. Weber defines value-relevance as an expression of the fact that science must selectively concentrate upon those aspects of empirical reality that make it "worth knowing." Hence, Weber writes, "the perception of the meaningfulness [to us] of [some slice of] empirically conditioned phenomena is what we presuppose for its becoming an object of investigation."[27] Weber evidently considers this "relation to values" indispensable if cultural inquiry is to be non-reductionistic, that is, if it is to be independently concerned with problems of meaning. This is crucial if the impetus toward ethically meaningful self-control in science can transcend mere decisionism. In this connection he tries to show why the aim of a science dedicated to the study of cultural meaning is to 'individualize' empirical data rather than to produce valid generalizations about the causes of behaviour:

> Firstly because the knowledge of social laws is not knowledge of social reality but rather one of the various aids used by our minds for attaining this end; secondly, because knowledge of cultural events is inconceivable except on the basis of significations which the concrete constellation of reality have for us in certain individual concrete situations. In which case and in which situations this is the case is not revealed to us by any law; it is decided according to value-ideas in the light of which we view "culture" in each individual case.[28]

On the basis of this passage there would seem to be good reason to question whether Weber can consistently project a moral horizon for scientific rationalists, for he also insists that the presuppositions about the value of those truths (the findings) acquired in any investigation of empirical reality ultimately have a subjective basis.[29]

It does, however, appear that Weber was acknowledging just this

---

Ethics and Methods, p. 58.

[27] "Objectivity," p. 79.

[28] Ibid., p. 80.

[29] For the clearest account of these inconsistencies in Weber's work see Guy Oakes, "Rickert's Value Theory and the Foundations of Weber's Methodology," pp. 38–51.

problem when, in his famous essay "Science as a Vocation," he spoke of the possibility of science lacking any intrinsic meaning. He states there that the "existence of science" does not bring "an increased and general knowledge of the conditions under which one lives." Rather, according to the thesis of the "disenchantment" of the world, science can only offer us, in the realm of the external conditions of action, circumstances under which our deliberate actions can be tailored to, and augmented by, calculable operations. In this respect, it substitutes contingently useful hypotheses for the search for intrinsic meaning.[30] Weber was aware that in an age of "subjectivist culture" this was not an insight that would give solace to his audience or especially to those looking for the kind of social theory (the kind he called 'prophesies') which could give intrinsic meaning to the struggles of practical life, or an objective guide to the historical choices to be made.[31]

However, the case could be made that Weber does go beyond 'ethical neutrality' taken in the narrow sense that science must be silent about the question of what values one should live for. Accordingly, Weber wanted to examine the possibilities of elaborating a modern ethos suited to the disenchanted world. In this context, value neutrality itself seems to designate a specialized way of living for one's values. In this way of resolving the antagonism between science and politics, unique problems in the design of Weber's *oeuvre* come to the fore. Portis has suggested that Weber's work itself must be read in terms of his failed attempt to make the demand to separate the two realms personally consistent:

> Politics and science are incompatible ways by which behaviour can be rendered consistent with ultimate values. The most significant capabilities incorporated into Weber's self-concept were those appropriate to science, but the value that gave focus to his scientific activity, and therefore the most important functional aspect of his identity, was politics. In other words, Weber was committed to a type of activity in which he could not be

---

[30] "Science as a Vocation," p 139–38.

[31] On the theme of subjectivist culture in Weber's work see Scaff, "Politics in the 'Age of Subjectivist Culture': Weber's Thematic of the Modern," Paper delivered at American Political Science Association Meetings, September, 1987. The term is from Weber's address given in Vienna in 1909.

active...Although his aptitude for science was developed in his youth as a response to definite needs [financial independence], his commitment to politics was a logical consequence of his social thought.[32]

Leaving aside the otherwise important biographical questions, it is instructive to see what is at stake here for the interpretation of Weber's work as a whole. We are driven to consider whether, in view of Weber's conception of the independence of science from politics (as the sphere of struggle and irreconcilable value-conflict), there can be any *rapprochement* at all between his perspective and liberalism's commitment to social and political rationality.

CRITICAL RATIONALISM AS A MODEL OF LIBERAL MORALITY

Schluchter has made the interesting suggestion that not only is the 'independence' of the scientist's ultimate attitude important for Weber but so is, in institutional terms, the scientist's "freedom to relate to politics." Schluchter proposes that

Autonomy means more than differentiation. After all there is role differentiation, too, between the civil servant and the politician. Autonomy means first of all freedom from political interference ... but [the scientist] also confronts politics with the value position of science. Freedom from practical value judgement defines not only the limits of science but also its cultural claim.[33]

With this interpretation the objectivity of knowledge would then refer to the role science can play in society as a whole when it promotes, as Weber had hoped, both the decision-maker's search for "clarity" in questions of meaning and the readiness to acknowledge disappointing facts in the various activities of work and life. This, according to Schluchter, is the most promising development of Weber's famous "ethics of responsibility." As we shall see, Schluchter's qualifications of Weber's view of science ultimately depend on his belief that there is

---

[32] Portis, *Max Weber and Political Commitment*, pp. 108, 111.

[33] Schluchter, "Value-neutrality and the Ethic of Responsibility," in *Max Weber's Vision of History*, p. 103.

a more promising side of Weber's thought for developing moral-political understandings of modern society which Weber himself seemed to mistakenly cut off. Insisting on Weber's misreading of his own disenchantment thesis, Schluchter (in an analogous way to Habermas) is led to conclude that Weber's work "shows us the reasons for our discontent with modernity, but it also makes clear why we will do well not to give in to this discontent." But perhaps even more appropriately we read a few pages earlier that if Weber is to provide a satisfactory outline for a specifically modern ethos we must be "ready to argue in his own terms against him."[34]

Schluchter believes that this is possible so long as we see that Weber's ethic of responsibility expresses certain imperatives science shares with politics. He wants to develop the idea of the critical function of science as the neglected side of Weber's more sceptical claim that science cannot pretend to decipher the meaning of human struggles and must confine itself to helping actors to distil practical issues into choices among conflicting ultimate values. But here another problem in Weber's own analysis emerges: the role of scientific knowledge in the definition and eventual solution to practical problems is marked by the dual role it plays in relation to basic institutional components of modern society. Here he claims that one must not absolutize the distinction between the possible contribution of science to the cultural self-awareness of actors and the indispensability of science for technical problem-solving. But relating these two roles seems difficult if one insists, as Weber did, that the scientist cannot criticize the demands of any given ultimate understanding of reality except with regard to the agent's own understanding of the costs and realizability of his or her aims in practical life.

Weber implies that the politically responsible actor must know where argument ends and commitment begins. He believed that for the scientist, however, service to moral forces could be maintained only by opening the necessarily pointed questions being addressed to criticism and provocation. Weber implies, of course, that the politician could be convinced of the importance of promoting such openness as a social

---

[34] Schluchter, "The Paradox of Rationalization" in *Max Weber's Vision of History*, pp. 59, 53.

value even though openness could not be regarded by her as an autonomous norm of political action itself. The politician must keep in mind the Machiavellian distinction between what the value of openness demands as a principle and what it means to be responsible for the political success of openness in society.

The only way of reconstructing Weber's thought in a way that recovers an enlightenment conception of public reason is by showing how the value-demand to expose one's beliefs to the severest possible criticism could be generalized in an effective way beyond science. To do this one can no longer understand the exercise of intellectual integrity in the way Weber did. Habermas, for instance, has tried to show that the 'moral service' apparently preserved for science by the notion of intellectual integrity is itself deliberately limited when Weber understands it exclusively in the context of finding an antidote to "illusory rationalizations of politics" entailed by the necessarily irrational substance of public opinion.[35] Weber focused so singlemindedly upon freeing the use of the lecture hall from cheap concessions to undisciplined mass feelings, that he cut off completely the possibility of the critical functioning of a dialogue between the realm of expertise and the realm of politics. According to Schluchter and Habermas this is why Weber arrived at an ultimately positivist separation of science from the sephere of practice. As Habermas put it, Weber had to ultimately side with positivism as a natural consequence of his assumption that in modern society "political will" can no longer be enlightened.[36] He did not see that one merely pre-empts 'enlightenment' in so far as one assumes the irredeemable irrationality of public life. One must then favour the technocratic model of decision, or democracy hijacked by elites, by default—that is, as the only available model of political rationalization (even if it is a self-defeating one) for modern societies.[37]

In order to counter Weber's decisionism Schluchter has suggested that there is an affinity to Popperian 'critical rationalism' that

---

[35] Habermas, *Toward a Rational Society*, p. 69.

[36] Ibid., pp. 69-70.

[37] For a detailed discussion of this problem see Warren, "Max Weber's Liberalism for a Nietzschean World."

unfortunately remained only implicit in Weber. In particular, Schluchter turns to Karl Popper's pupil, Hans Albert, who has explicitly argued that Weber's theory of science presupposes a solution to the problem of rationality quite at variance to the one which he explicitly elaborated.[38] Albert states that Weber's view of science quite obviously contains an aspiration to distinguish between mere calculability or prediction on the one hand, and, on the other, conscious action. Where Weber went wrong was in suggesting that the receptivity of politics to the claims of scientific reason can go no further than the ability to control or foresee all of the relevant consequences of action. Weber did not see that the attitude of responsibility—that is, being prepared to engage in the never completed attempt to imagine the intended and unintended consequences of possible decisions—is itself linked to a demand of moral consciousness in liberal society. Unfortunately, Weber simply limited the scope of critical arguments in science to examining the consistency of different value standpoints.[39]

Following Popper, Albert claims that Weber failed to overcome his dependence upon a classical conception of rationality—the principle of sufficient justification—in which a theory aims at an axiomatization, or the evidential justification of some 'given' set of claims. In the end Weber could escape the strict version of this conception only by his neo-Kantian assumption that our ultimate conceptions of reality are necessarily impervious to critique. However he thereby fails to see that the meaning of science itself lies in prefiguring and sustaining the moral ideal of liberal societies, namely, the commitment to the capacity of reason to dissolve 'dogmatizations' that are socially stabilized for ideological reasons.

Both Weber and critical rationalism are in agreement that science is a uniquely creative way of exposing debate to the "stimulus of practical problems," to use Popper's words.[40] Both claim that, when constructing a theory, there is no way of eliminating subjective presuppositions and value-laden expectations about what the meaning of the findings will be.

---

[38] Hans Albert, *Treatise on Critical Reason*, p. 98.

[39] Ibid., p. 90.

[40] Popper, *The Poverty of Historicism*; This conception is very close to that of Weber, in "Objectivity," p. 61.

Yet Popper takes pains to show that it does make a great deal of difference whether, in the 'decisions' underlying a theory, one is following the rule of choosing the theory most likely to be accepted on the basis of currently available evidence or the one most worthy of further critical discussion.[41] Popper's conclusion here is well-known: even if ultimately subjective decisions are necessary in theory formation, it is still possible, in principle, to view the task of science as the propagation of those decisions which would have the most promise when it comes to "learning from our mistakes." It is not the aim of truly rational institutions to realize the liberating idea but rather to combat dogmatizations and guarantee inclusive discussion and membership. In this sense science plays a leading role in sponsoring modern society's institutional expression of moral development. It is therefore suited to liberalism's indirect promotion of moral growth and maturity through the pacification of conflict and controversy.

According to this idea the relationship of science to politics is not limited to increasing our ability to act rationally in a given means-ends continuum. Rather, a different view of rationality is outlined when one explores the methodological implications of the force of 'criticism,' which designates a kind of principled openness to the possible challenges posed by the alternative arguments of others. The social and political potential of critical rationalism is not realized by a radical separation from morality; instead morality would be realized in the attempt to make commitment to an enlightened critical stance within science practically effective for society as a whole. Morality would be based on testing the extent to which the limits to rationality that do exist are imposed by the refusal to have one's fundamental beliefs criticized.[42] As Albert puts it, the real moral and political vocation of science would consist in replacing the "will to certitude" with

> the will to attain solutions that remain open to possible criticism—solutions subject to resistance from both reality and from other members of society, which must either prove themselves or come to grief in the process. The closing of systems of belief is not a command of logic or any other objective

---

[41] Popper, *Conjectures and Refutations*, p. 218n.
[42] Schluchter, "Value-neutrality and the Ethic of Responsibility," p. 109.

authority: it is a demand of the will and of the demands and interests that stand behind it. The openness of such systems, one might well say, is itself a moral question.

Critical rationalism starts from the assumption that rationality and progress in society requires the commitment to a systematic openness to alternative problem definitions. Weber's project could be made compatible with this position if one emphasizes his belief that intellectual integrity is promoted when it is stimulated by the willingness to gather the most "uncomfortable" facts about the world. This shows the need, as Habermas also insists, to counter Weber's assumption that science must be considered independent of the handling of concrete political issues—for the sake of integrity itself! In this conception it is unnecessary to cut off politics from the distinctive moral challenge that could be said to follow from responsible commitment to science as a value.[43]

Despite criticisms that Habermas had earlier levelled at Popper and his 'school' they are basically in agreement about the importance of open social institutions and receptivity to provocative ideas in 'serious' argumentation. Perhaps their most conspicuous agreement lies in the idea that intersubjectively achieved understandings can be rational only if the relevant discursive participants can view their prior attachments to beliefs and practices as contingent. Popper argues that the possibility of producing rational knowledge depends upon our ability to identify meaningful controversy, or our willingness to enter "fruitful" discussions. But here Popper has been justly criticized for assuming that the capacity for identifying a meaningful controversy or fruitful discussion is somehow not a controversial part of the very discursive situation of critical argument itself.[44]

H.T. Wilson has pointed to the roots of these problems of Popper's

---

[43] Cf. "The Meaning of 'Ethical Neutrality'," p. 13, where Weber writes: "What we must vigorously oppose is the view that one may be 'scientifically' contented with the conventional self-evidentness of very widely accepted value judgements. The specific function of science, it seems to me, is just the opposite: namely, to ask questions about these things which convention makes self-evident."

[44] For an excellent discussion of this issue in the debate between Popper and his critics see Bernstein, *Beyond Objectivism and Relativism*, p. 79.

theory. Popper admits that a theory of scientific progress is necessary if one is to show how it is the advancement of truth, rather than a contingent agreement on what will count as truth, that takes place through the action and discussion whose very output is the development of the criteria of science. Wilson shows how, for Popper, the search for truth really takes place only indirectly, that is by the formation of the right kind of community—the community of science—in which the procedures guaranteeing "openness" would be operational. The real fault of Popper's therefore lies in his giving science a monopoly over the search for truth by default. Science is given its legitimacy as a neutral, benign way of processing controversies only because of its non-neutral role in certain kinds of social projects (organized around norms of functional rationality) upon which the hopes of rationality are presumed to depend.[45]

For Wilson, Weber is different from Popper only because the separation between theory and practice, science and politics was recognized by him as resulting from, and exposing the limits of, his own conception of rationality. In Wilson's reading, however, the blindspot of Weber's view of science consists in his proceding from the assumption that the meaninglessness of science and rationality itself affords a superior insight into human possibilities, requiring no attempt to oppose, in practice, the contingent world he occupied. In doing so Weber is content to conflate the domestication of human possibility with the limits of reason. Weber endorses a point of departure with which he himself could not identify: the reduction of value-rational action to a formalizable problem, an axis of meaningful action to be distinguished as an object of empirical research.[46]

In Popper, the process of scientific progress (towards truth) proceeds as if by natural selection, ensuring that the only socially effective committment that issues from science will be that which follows from the falsification process itself. This assumes, however, that only responsibility, or always provisional problem-solving, rather than truth, can remain as the standard for intervention in practical affairs where, after all, participants are faced with decisions rather than

---

[45] Wilson, *The American Ideology*, chs. 4 and 5.
[46] Wilson, "Reading Max Weber: The Limits of Sociology," pp. 306–7.

hypotheses.[47] In this sense Popper makes the disenchantment of the world safe for liberal democratic normative culture. Indeed, Popper makes a virtue of the split between theory and practice or science and politics where Weber had seen this as the fate connected with the disenchantment of the world.

Wilson shows how the very notion of theory informing this model of science must remain infinitely distant from substantive or practical rationality. Ultimately Weber and Popper uncritically accede to a world in which theory can only make a difference to practice when its goal in the latter area is that of success, not truth. This is because only an empirical social science tailored to piecemeal social engineering remains qualified to control value-informed choices in a responsible way. Social science must offer itself as a social technology for testing social directions through value-neutral and incremental disappointment-monitoring.[48] Social science would therefore remain indifferent to the distinction between the critical role of theory on the one hand, and the moral-political project of challenging empirically accepted interests and motives. The result is that critically informed practice becomes hostaged to "the rules of a game which themselves demand critical scrutiny."[49]

If, as Popper claims, rationality in an "open society" can never be independent of 'decision,' his notion of rationality itself is placed in question. He has resisted the idea that fallibilism is in need of a substantive defense. This has prompted Habermas to argue that

> Popper over-extends the methodological power of the negative with his theory of falsification, and makes the critical method of refutation autonomous...In consequence he denies himself the possibility of validating criticism itself as a rational activity. For Popper criticism is ultimately just one option among others. He is forced to rely on a decision for rationality, on a critical attitude, a readiness to engage in criticism, and on the traditions that presuppose such a disposition. I believe I can show that a species that depends for its survival on the structures of linguistic communication and

---

[47] *The American Ideology*, pp. 108ff.
[48] Wilson, "Critical Theory's Critique of Social Science: Episodes in a changing Problematic from Adorno to Habermas, Part II," p. 299.
[49] Wilson, *The American Ideology*, p. 36.

cooperative, purposive rational action, must of necessity rely on reason. In the validity claim, however implicit, by means of which we are obliged to orient ourselves in our communicative actions, a persistent, albeit repeatedly suppressed, claim of reason lies concealed.[50]

In short, critical theorists like Habermas and Wilson show that the decisionistic complacency regarding the link between theory and practice which Weber could not avoid has not been purged by critical rationalism either.[51] This demonstrates the need to find correctives to Weber's and Popper's tendency to pre-empt what Wilson calls the "rationality of practice." Habermas' theory of communicative rationality is just such an attempt.

COMMUNICATIVE ACTION AS A NEGLECTED ETHICAL PERSPECTIVE

As we have seen Habermas claims that Weber not only surrenders to the alternative between cultural elitism and functional-technocratic rationality in politics but also to a decisionistic dogmatism of belief that limits the practical aspiration towards a rational telos of social understanding. The reason, he argues, is that Weber lacked a theoretical perspective that would have allowed him to see that the promise of modern ideals depends, in the first instance, upon whether they can be reconstructed according to the rational potential of "communicative action." This is ironic, according to Habermas, because Weber's social theory itself can be used to show that this potential has been short-circuited by one-sided developments like bureaucratization and the rise of functional rationality, and not by a fatal flaw of modernity, which has led to the impoverishment of the modern "life-world."[52] Weber failed to see that we do not establish access to the world of cultural meaning simply as teleological acting subjects whose more or less clearly elaborated beliefs and goals are ultimately

---

[50] Habermas, *Autonomy and Solidarity: Interviews with Jürgen Habermas*, ed. P. Dews, p. 51.

[51] In this context he points to Apel's criticisms of Popper, Albert and others. See K.O. Apel "The Problem of Philosophical Foundations in Light of a Transcendental Pragmatics of Language," in *After Philosophy*, ed. T. McCarthy.

[52] Habermas, *Theory of Communicative Action*, vol. 2, ch. 8.

questions of "faith." The autonomy of a teleological actor can only be secured through strategic objectification of others or through the expression of power interests. Culture and socialization must be reduced to the status of implicit means of power unless access to meaning can be shown to depend, at least potentially, on genuinely cooperative achievements involving consensual coordination of beliefs and goals.

In Habermas' view of 'life-world relations,' or communicative action, the stakes that individuals attach to their action cannot be understood solely from the perspective of the possible conflict or forced harmonization of their ultimately subjective positions. Weber's moral scepticism was largely based on the idea that the irreconcilability of values is implicit in the nature of social existence, and that modern societies simply highlight it more dramatically. As such, he believed that even if the nihilistic implications of subjectivism could be overcome by individual personalities the truly creative sources of meaning and commitment could only be achieved in a social form by historically or charismatically appealing images of the ultimate problems of reality. Such sources of meaning cannot, in principle, be opened to rational criticism.

Habermas suggests, however, that there is a dimension of social action which is independently coordinated by the attempt to "reach an understanding" and which therefore has its own non-subjectivistic criterion of success or failure. He argues that the theory of communicative action shows that the kind of agreement that is achieved through a successful attempt to reach an understanding is different from an agreement that comes about through successful strategic action or attempts to 'influence.'[53] Habermas argues that human reality involves problems and controversies that cannot be seriously addressed except through actions which are pursued with a communicative intent, and that this is true not only of 'rational will-formation' in public life, but perhaps even more especially in child rearing and socialization as well as education. Even the modern 'life-world,' which is divided into disparate spheres of social meaning and validity, still requires human

---

[53] Habermas, *The Theory of Communicative Action*, vol. 1, ch. 3.

beings to elaborate the conditions of its basic integrity through its communicative infrastructure. It is obvious here that Habermas has not only Weber as his main antagonist, but also the tradition of thinkers—from Nietzsche, through Heidegger and Adorno—who either question the basic integrity of the modern life-world or find it inaccessible to any perspective except a philosophical aestheticism or elitism.[54]

But for our present purposes it is important to see that communicative action, in Habermas' sense, must be appreciated for its potential to foster normative demands—irreducible to those of strategic action—upon the rational development of social institutions and procedures. For instance we can take as an example the recognition of a norm which, to be effective, must have an intersubjectively binding effect. According to Habermas' theory this binding quality must be brought about with at least some reference to the manner in which 'life-world relations' are regulated by "communicative intentions." If, by contrast, one remained within the bounds of classical, Lockean liberalism then social arrangements would be considered legitimate when they secure the ability of individuals to pursue independently their own purposes and idea of the good without arbitrary constraint. Yet it has become apparent that the types of arrangements which are supposed to provide free, reliable and inclusive access to the means of effective teleological action have actually produced institutions and attitudes which have undermined the process of moral-practical rationalization for which they were originally designed. The functioning of these institutions and attitudes involves the maintenance of social relations based one-sidedly on property, occupational hierarchy, subjectivization of rights and entitlements and public passivity. They are therefore associated with privatized conceptions of individual fulfilment tailored to the market and trends toward bureaucratization that destroy the communicative infrastructure upon which the original ethical meanings of liberal enlightenment culture were to be based.

Habermas claims, however, that our image of a good society can be

---

[54] Of course Habermas has criticized this tradition on the grounds that it fails to develop an alternative to the "subject-centered" conception of rationality characteristic of post-Hegelian philosophy. See Habermas, *The Philosophical Discourse of Modernity*.

based on a reconstruction of the liberal solution under which the legitimacy of political and social arrangements depends upon the acceptance of principles upon which rationally autonomous individuals can agree. It is Kantian liberalism that he seeks to restore. Yet Habermas knows that moral controversy cannot be rationally solved by John Rawls' method of having otherwise egotistical individuals place themselves under a "veil of ignorance" in which they are constrained to act as if they had an interest in following an impartial procedure for adjudicating their competing claims. This solution obviously requires the participants who are to agree upon basic principles of justice to bracket their subjective attachments, implying a supplemental agreement to be placed in the so-called "original position" in the first place.[55] Habermas wants rather to define the very motivations for the search for an agreement as rooted in the ability of human beings to learn how to solve problems cooperatively through consensus, rather than on the basis of what hypothetical participants would do if they had to cooperate. Unlike Rawls, Habermas stresses the communicative competence of participants, rather than a theoretically convenient foundation of cooperation in consistent self-interest.[56]

This is where his theory of 'communicative rationality' enters the picture. Communicative rationality, even though it involves presuppositions it cannot make fully conscious, and risks of disagreement which it cannot control, does not require that practical reasoners must share certain basic values. Rather it proposes that even those who have a different view of the society in which they would like to live, if they want to "argue seriously," must be willing to reconsider what they count as a reason for accepting or rejecting a claim to normative validity.[57] Such abstraction from subjective perspectives is always already anticipated by reflective actors taking part in consensually coordinated action since consistently playing by the rules of this type of action reveals to participants that they are constrained by a standard of success or failure that lies outside the dimension of strategic action. One need not make a prior decision in favour of the intrinsic

---

[55] Habermas, "Justice and Solidarity," p. 37.

[56] Habermas, *Moral Consciousness and Communicative Action*, p. 66–67.

[57] Habermas, "Law and Morality," p. 243.

desirability of social relations free of strategic objectification of social partners or adversaries.

In this respect Habermas claims that an appeal to idealized conditions of free argumentation is possible which would merely extend, and not violate, "prior embeddedness in intersubjectively shared forms of life."[58] He admits that not every community is constituted by explicit acceptance of the norms of conversational equality and fairness that he has in mind. Nevertheless he argues that any constraints that are imposed by the requirement to universalize one's interests and abstract from contingent value-commitments in a hypothetically designed discussion among equals are only those which reflective, responsible members of particular forms of life reciprocally and unavoidably presuppose when they engage in dispute settlements through argumentation. He claims that in a modern, post-traditional and rationalized culture morality is pushed toward the problem of universalization and argument-mediated discussion purely by the "increasing reflexivity of cultural traditions." Yet this implies that judgements about the compelling nature of universalizing claims within a particular form of life would not have to be based on a decision to favour certain formal norms of moral cooperation.[59]

Weber proposed that intellectual integrity in science or an ethics of responsibility in politics could be fostered as distinctive ways of living for one's values in a disenchanted world where ethical meaning is established by the way one happens to live or the kind of conscious choices one makes. By contrast, Habermas dramatizes his appeal to the possibility of cognitive testing of validity claims by the unavoidable, though often "suppressed" idea, of the 'unforced force of the best argument.' Hence he drops any requirement that the ideal of a rational society must be grounded in commitment to an ultimate standard. Weber, on the other hand, dramatized his sceptical view of reason by his claim that only political and scientific practices that were more genuinely aware of cultural contingencies could develop and withstand a tragic consciousness of the conflict of ultimate value positions.

---

[58] "Justice and Solidarity," p. 49; *Autonomy and Solidarity*, p. 184.

[59] On these and other points see the essay by Steven Lukes, "Of Gods and Demons," in *Habermas: Critical Debates*, ed. J. Thompson.

In arriving at his controversial account of modernity Weber did not necessarily endorse either irrationality in politics or an absolute independence of rational endeavour from political life. Rather he was simply guided by the insight that ideals like "modern freedom presupposed a certain conjunction of unique and unrepeatable conditions"[60] which he now believed were no longer effective. 'Deontological' liberals like Habermas and Rawls try to elaborate a conception of modern ideals which is grounded in the abstract, "de-centered" social identity of modern societies and their members. Habermas in particular insists that the perspective of "ideal role taking" necessary for undistorted communication corresponds to "universal intuitions" regarding justice built into the formal conditions of contexts of moral learning. But is it necessarily true that we can know in advance that we are in a situation calling for action with a communicative intent in which we unavoidably presuppose ideal speech? Habermas has indeed shown that the telos of rational communicative action—where it is "pragmatically" necessary that validity claims are under consideration—can be conceived along the lines of an ideal context of interaction. But he has not shown that mature and reflective political actions and decisions must be informed by this ideal.

Against this, Michael Walzer, himself a liberal, has suggested that perhaps our political enlightenment will come from an awareness that our reasons and designs for seeking freer discussions and a more equitable society must always precede ideal speech rather than emerge from it.[61] Indeed, he and other crtitics of Habermas have argued that politics involves the task of making social choices, and empowering certain kinds of people, or re-examining our "identity-needs," in a way that cannot be as subject to impartial judgement as can the purified intentions and validity claims of participants in an ideal communication community.[62] By his own admission, Habermas' criteria of rational moral judgement cannot be fulfilled unless we are prepared to accept

---

[60] Weber, "Prospects for Liberal Democracy in Tsarist Russia," *Selections in Translation*, p. 282.

[61] Walzer, "A Critique of Philosophical Conversation," p. 194.

[62] These problems are reviewed with great acumen in Alessandro Ferrara, "A Critique of Habermas' *Diskursethik*."

outcomes which "provide demotivated answers to decontextualized questions."[63]   Although in his social theory he deplores the "colonization of the life-world" by decontextualized goods, his ethical theory appeals to an ideal that has the power to transcend the "naive validity of the context of the life world."[64] In Habermas' view the goals of morality can never be the same as the goals of politics since we cannot accept them on the basis of who we are, or who we might turn out to be, as a result of applying them.

In his later work Habermas acknowledges that even if our model of justice were to be informed by the ideal speech community, in which the rules of the game are neutral and impartial, it is impossible for the rules of the game in any society to be neutral and impartial toward all kinds of moral aspirations and identity-forming contexts.[65] Discursive fairness and impartiality may be the best way of cooperatively testing our communicative intentions and validity claims, but the goals of politics are never simply definable in terms of perfecting cooperation.[66] Habermas knows that the Kantian lineage of his theory appears to obscure the discrepancy between the ideal itself and the actual substantive conditions and results of applying it. Against the "sceptics," however, he argues that an ethic of responsibility would simply be one way in which his "discourse ethics" would incorporate sensitivity to unintended consequences into the aspiration to achieve rational justice.[67] But the proponent of an ethic of principle like Habermas must admit that the purity of morality is the source of its value; it takes precedence over other values only by this fact, not because it thereby eliminates other, contingent sources of value. This is why Bernard Williams has said that ethical theories do better when they clarify the specific social function of morality—including its ability to make us aware of contingent inequality and effects of power (which, at its best, Habermas' work does)—rather than advancing a claim to put us beyond political controversy and

---

[63] Habermas, *Moral Consciousness and Communicative Action*, p. 106.

[64] Ibid., p. 109.

[65] Ibid., pp. 102–4, 195–211.

[66] For a similar argument see Cornelius Castoriadis, *Philosophy, Politics and Autonomy: Essays in Political Philosophy*, p. 77ff.

[67] Ibid., p. 106, 206.

"luck" in our ethical aspirations. If the value of all our ethical aspirations were to rest upon the self-sufficiency of morality, then we would need a source of value that consists "not only in trying rather than succeeding, since success depends partly on luck, but in a kind of trying that lies beyond the level at which the capacity to try can itself be a matter of luck." What Williams is saying, and it often seems to apply to Habermas, is that, unless we can specify in advance the conditions under which cooperation and communication can be rational, then all empirical agreements and socially successful forms of moral belief must be viewed simply as possible tools of manipulation and power.[68] In the next chapters I will take up the work of Strauss and Rorty who propose a different way of coping with the intellectual dilemma that "our" moral goals might only be defensible in light of the consequences of their cultural "success."

---

[68] Bernard Williams, *Ethics and the Limits of Philosophy*, pp. 194–5.

Chapter Five

THE CRISIS OF LIBERALISM IN SOCIAL SCIENCE: STRAUSS ON WEBER

Leo Strauss' critical essay on Weber is found in the second chapter of *Natural Right and History*, his most well-known book on political philosophy. Strauss argues that, in the work of Weber, the greatest representative of modern social science, we have a particularly vivid example of the consequences of modern philosophy's immoderate conquest of classical rationalism. Most importantly Strauss wants to show how Weber's science presupposes the victory of positivist or Cartesian science[1] and its radical break with prescientific knowledge (opinions about moral and political authority). Weber's thought is a symptom of the "dogmatic scepticism" of the historicist direction of modern philosophy which contrasts with classical rationalism's prudent respect for the tension between systems of conventional right and systems of natural right. Strauss argues that the Weberian inquirer who follows the maxim of separating facts and values appears to do so in the name of a "non-evaluating objectivity," which is directly opposed to the richer conception of objectivity (rooted in common sense) as classical political philosophy had developed it.

INTELLECTUAL INTEGRITY:
ENNOBLING THE RETREAT FROM REASON

The basis of the transition from non-evaluative to evaluative thought is first addressed by Strauss' repeated claims that we cannot approach the

---

[1] Leo Strauss, *Natural Right and History*, p. 78–9.

phenomena of human excellence with the methods or insights of empirical social science. Classical philosophy does not hesitate to characterize the life of human excellence or goodness as the most successful or most pleasurable life. Philosophers became political philosophers when they challenged particular societies to question their own images of success or goodness by becoming open to the idea of natural success or goodness. The classical philosophers believed that knowledge of nature provides the only hope for establishing universal or even relevant standards in this area. But modern or non-teleological modes of philosophizing deny that one can arrive at criteria for the morally successful life or good life according to natural standards. As a result it becomes possible to see the moral or political influence of ideals of human goodness or excellence as merely a function of the ways in which individuals or groups have tried to bring about a way of life which will fulfil their system of needs or preferences. Strauss abhors this materialist understanding of culture (which is supposed to be progressive) which "forces its holders to understand the higher as nothing but the effect of the lower, or which prevents them from considering the possibility that there are phenomena which are simply irreducible to their conditions, that there are phenomena that form a class by themselves."[2]

Strauss seems to concede that Weber is not a materialist in the normal sense. Indeed Weber's ideal types can in no way be said to provide the basis for a materialist or deterministic account of historically influential ideals or constellations of interests. But Weber's conclusion is that if we want to analyze social reality with concepts that have independently normative significance we must presuppose the "ephemeral validity" of those very concepts.[3] As we shall see, Strauss draws our attention to Weber's refusal or inability to pose the question of the good society despite his attempt to make non-reductionist historical understanding the basis of social science.[4]

---

[2] Ibid., pp. 128–9.
[3] Ibid., pp. 55–58.
[4] Strauss, "What is Political Philosophy," in *An Introduction to Political Philosophy*, ed. H. Gilden, pp. 22–3; See also the remarks by Allan Bloom, Strauss' leading student, on Weber's commendable anti-reductionism in "Raymond Aron: The Last

Strauss notes that Weber shares the adherence of modern social science to "method," rather than to evaluative reason. This primacy of method compels social science to radically dissociate what it calls 'objectivity' from the commitments of adherents to particular value systems, or ideologies.[5] It is only on this basis that social science can erect its sham claim that it can achieve an insight into the true nature of all value systems which makes it uniquely qualified to illuminate them from an objective standpoint. In the end, Weber shows that one can avoid reductionist thinking only by means of the distinction between facts and values.

Weber, of course, believed that social science helps us clarify and explain the way commitments to values have influenced the horizon of human action. But under the assumptions of historicism to which Weber still clung, every social scientific truth is bounded by contingency because it is first stimulated by a culturally limited interest. At best the knower can try to gain an appreciation of a given culture by attaining a sympathetic, non-reductionist attitude toward the meaning-elements of 'individualized,' ideal-typical, patterns of development by which that culture is constituted. Because it presupposes the imposs-ibility of a privileged view of the irreducible value contents of life, historicism dispels the possibility of teleological interpretations of culture. Indeed, no truth about culture can have the status of knowledge unless it is the truth about truth—that is, unless it is based on the insight that all effective cultural ideals or values are themselves more or less influential forms of self-justification. In Strauss' terms social science begins not only with respect for the conventionality of all influential ideals, but also with the philosophically polemical assertion that it is foolish to believe that conventional truths could ever be transcended by the truths of nature, that is, by the discovery of what is best and highest in human life.

Of course, as any reader of Strauss is aware, much of the blame is to be laid at the hands of the founders of modern thought who interpreted nature as 'necessity' or saw nature as a lost original state

---

of the Liberals," in his *Giants and Dwarfs*, p. 261.

[5] See especially Strauss' essays "What is Political Philosophy" and "An Epilogue," in *An Introduction to Political Philosophy*.

which humanity tries to regain through a supplement called 'culture' (Rousseau) or through acts of self-overcoming (Nietzsche). As a result, Strauss argues, what is most distinctive about modern reason is that it cannot identify itself with 'wisdom.' In fact, Weberian social science, or historical sociology, can only differentiate the possible overt responses or adaptations to historically unique situations and permit one to determine, through what Weber called "individualization", whether and how such responses or adaptations are consistent (or inconsistent) with a given or constructed form of self-justification. Reason cannot claim to provide superior understanding of values, if this means supplying criteria for defending the values or ideals in the name of which a culture is formed. The very concept of "culture," Strauss implies, has the effect of reducing questions of the truth of values or ideals to means for enhancing a society's sense of identity or justifying the advantages of its way of life to its members. But Strauss adds, "What we now call culture is the accidental result of concerns that were not concerns with culture but with other things and above all with the Truth."[6]

Implicit in social scientific rationality—which Strauss deplores as the reigning self-understanding of liberal culture—is a kind of relativist drift, and this relativism is not simply of epistemological significance but implies a specifically modern form of justice. The justice of intellectuals is the mandate for what we now call 'political correctness' whereby the dignity of each culture is held to be diminished whenever one fails to grant its right to seek its singular identity or self-understood advantage on its own. Indeed Strauss, and later his leading protégé, Allan Bloom, raged against the kinship between liberal democracy and relativism, not, they claim, because their cause is anti-liberal, but because they feared that respect for culture was blindly prevailing over genuine philosophy in contemporary liberal democracies. Strauss argues that although social science claims it does not intend to formulate a comparison of values themselves (and can only compare the types of influence they have had) its view of the necessity of the fact/value distinction really grows out of one culture's view of the problem of culture.

---

[6] Strauss, *Studies in Platonic Political Philosophy*, p. 149.

We have seen that critical rationalism and Weber believe that the ultimate development of modern scientific reason can only come to light once it is admitted that the validity of values can never be finally established by reason alone.   Strauss' concern is to show that this is the back door through which modern intellectuals advance their claim to have finally arrived at the ultimate goal of the theoretical life, namely, intellectual integrity.   Strauss argues that the standard of intellectual integrity ultimately boils down to appreciation for diversity per se, and it cannot help but end in surrender to a relativism which, against its best intentions, actually devalues the theoretical approach itself.

Can social science then be an independent investigation of human problems?   In the name of openness, or intellectual integrity, it sees the value-beliefs of all cultures as equally unsupportable in their claims to be absolutely true.   As a consequence its own autonomy consists, paradoxically, in propounding the equal rights of all prejudices. Once again, if it wants to pretend that with this insight it has discovered what is universally true about culture, then social science itself cannot dissociate its own standard of objectivity from a rationally unexaminable preference for a certain kind of culture.[7]

Strauss indeed wonders how or whether Weber was convinced of the plausibility of the fact/value distinction.   Indeed Strauss points out that Weber had to be able to employ value judgements in order to investigate phenomena that are considered worthy of study.   For example, he had to employ, at least implicitly, categories of praise and disparagement, nobility and baseness, in order to distinguish prophets from charlatans, a distinction which proves crucial to the identification of religious phenomena in the first place.[8]   Weber thought he could maintain that value-neutral analysis applied to only one phase of inquiry; that is, while it is decisive for establishing the validity of the findings, it is not sufficient for identification of the problems, and therefore not for establishing the very goals of historical inquiry.   Thus Weber seems to assume that the distinction between value relevance and value judgements is sufficient to guarantee the integrity of his science.

---

[7] Strauss' most concise formulation of these points is found in "Relativism," in *Relativism and the Study of Man*, ed. H. Schoek and J. Wiggens.

[8] Strauss, *Natural Right and History*, p. 63-4.

Intellectual integrity means that the value commitments in the light of which we determine the questions to be asked in social science must be admitted to have their source, not in the facts themselves, but in our necessarily partial interest in the facts.[9]

There is an unmistakable link to Nietzsche here of which Strauss is acutely aware. The chapter preceding Strauss' critique of Weber deals with historicism and Nietzsche's relation to it. In the view of historicism all social phenomena are embedded within the struggle for interests and ideas which takes place within given patterns of development, or cultures, and whose ultimate meaning escapes purely rational judgement. To be sure, all human struggles and ideals involve a more or less explicit and effective belief in the validity of values and goals. However, each culture always puts forward an incomparable view of "the basic problems" which remains its own. As Strauss characterizes any such horizon: "it cannot be validated by reasoning, since it is the basis of reasoning."[10] In this sense, the fundamental premise of historicism is either that the basic problems cannot be solved or that the problems themselves are culturally relative.

Adherence to this premise, according to Strauss, means that historicism pre-empts the possibility of philosophy, the search for wisdom; if the basic problems change there does not remain any point at all in viewing the search for truth as the standpoint for understanding those who take themselves to be addressing those basic problems.[11] Moreover there is Nietzsche's recognition of the paradoxical nature of historicism. Historicism implies that theory can no longer be understood as the search for non-contingent truths. This involves the insight that since all truths are formed out of the non-neutral, affective dimension of human striving and will, theory and life (or commitment) itself are opposed to one another. According to Strauss, Nietzsche had to deal with the problem that independent thought requires the realization that one's thought cannot be independent. He therefore had to address the paradox of applying historicism as a theory to itself:

---

[9] Here we must recall Portis' claim (see chapter 4 above) that an interest in the facts cannot be placed beyond or above constituent features of identity and personality.

[10] *Natural Right and History*, p. 27.

[11] Ibid., pp. 20, 27, 38–9.

According to Nietzsche, the theoretical analysis of human life that realizes the relativity of all comprehensive views and thus depreciates them would make human life itself impossible, for it would destroy the protecting atmosphere within which life or culture or action is alone possible...To avert the danger to life, Nietzsche could choose one of two ways: he could insist on the strictly esoteric character of the theoretical analysis of life—that is, restore the Platonic notion of the noble delusion—or else he could deny the possibility of theory proper and so conceive of thought as essentially subservient to, or dependent on, life or fate. If not Nietzsche himself, at any rate his successors adopted the second alternative.[12]

As we shall see in the last section of this chapter, Strauss wants to show how the first option holds out the most promise for overcoming historicism.

Weber's notion of intellectual integrity is one of the strongest signs of his ties to historicism. At its core is the recognition that truth is relative to commitment, and that therefore those who seek intellectual integrity must at the same time undermine the attempt to relate the search for truth to the goal of attaining objective knowledge of the good. If the unqualified right to one's commitment is the legitimate basis of any moral-evaluative standpoint, then all action and speech addressing the conflict between competing value-positions can never be independent of the interests of power.[13] According to Strauss, if social science is marked by the goal of intellectual integrity, it is also legitimate to suspect social scientists of allowing their work to be used by those who have an unqualified right not to be committed to the truth.[14] Indeed Strauss argues that the crisis of liberal democracy reaches its most acute form when it becomes infected by the historicist's supposedly noble self-denial regarding the possibility of intellectually justifying beliefs.[15]

Strauss suggests that Weber thereby avoids acknowledgement of some inconvenient implications of his approach. Weber concedes that any kind of objectivity which is developed on the basis of historical understanding will bind the search for truth to the use of categories that

---

[12] Ibid., p. 26.
[13] Strauss, "Social Science and Humanism" in *The State of the Social Sciences*, ed. L. White, p. 423.
[14] Strauss, "What is Political Philosophy?," pp. 19–20.
[15] "An Epilogue," p. 148.

must be chosen for reasons that the theorist herself must recognize to be partial.[16] For example, Weber's choice of constructs, such as the three types of legitimate authority, is supposed to be a reflection of a theoretical commitment to illuminate the context within which we can examine the fate of certain modern values such as universal political freedom. At the very least this should have caused Weber to doubt whether cultural knowledge, as he sees it, can be objective, that is, whether the selective use of ideal types could ever provide a conceptual framework which permits *anyone* within a particular cultural perspective to gain clarity about his or her ties to certain important values and beliefs. In fact, Weber's own words display his posture of noble self-denial when he characterizes the term "value" as "that unfortunate child of misery of our science."[17]

As we have noted, Weber was well aware that within his own theory the objective meaning of socio-historical reality cannot be finally known, and can only come to light from the perspective of those values which we want to clarify for ourselves. Strauss claims that Weber is thereby unable to take seriously the main goal of his science, namely, that of "understanding." In particular, he fails to take other societies in their own terms. One can therefore conclude that

> since the self-interpretation of a society is an essential element of its being, he will not understand these societies as they really are. And since one cannot understand one's own society adequately if one does not understand other societies, he will not even be able to really understand his own society.[18]

Perhaps it is possible here to have recourse to a kind of 'Popperian' defense and the claim that objectivity in scientific method is not the same as the search for certainty in knowledge. Objectivity in knowledge is no more than the willingness to affirm fallibilism, or argumentative freedom, with its inevitable socio-political implications. This definition of objectivity is necessary if one wants to elaborate both

---

[16] *Natural Right and History*, p. 25.
[17] Weber, "Objectivity," p. 107.
[18] *Natural Right and History*, p. 56.

the risks and the possibilities for the growth and improvement of our cultural self-understanding while acknowledging the inevitably contingent choices facing one's society. Strauss, however, doubts that anyone could be prepared to take truth seriously so long as it is believed that rationality requires that we should not care whether we can know whether certain values—or 'our' values—matter more than others.

He argues that, at the very most, Weber shows how the true aim of objectivity is to produce a clarification of subjective judgement, an awareness of the equal rights to self-justification of one's own and other subjective standpoints. As such, the clarification of subjective judgement enables its addressees to become better aware of the costs and benefits of their ties to their prejudices. Every culture is a result of value choices resting upon some prejudice.[19] But if this is true then the ultimate character of its ideals would lie in the will to a given form of self-assertion: "The final formulation of Weber's ethical principle would thus be 'Thou shalt have preferences'—an Ought whose fulfilment is fully guaranteed by the Is."[20]

INTELLECTUAL CRISIS AND THE "SUCCESS" OF LIBERALISM

Strauss would no doubt argue that even if we suppose, with Jaspers and

---

[19] Herbert Marcuse made some of the same points in another context, in an essay known as a classic statement of the Frankfurt School's critique of instrumental and administrative rationality. He writes: "If in Weber's work the formal analysis of capitalism thus becomes the analysis of forms of domination, this is not due to a discontinuity in concept or method; their purity itself shows itself to be impure. And this is so, not because Max Weber was a bad or inconsistent sociologist, but because he knew his subject matter: Truth becomes critique and accusation, and accusation becomes the function of true science. If he subjected the science of economics to politics as early as in the inaugural address, this *tour de force* shows itself, in the light of the whole of Weber's work, as the inner logic of his method. Your science must remain 'pure'; only thus can you remain faithful to the truth. But this truth forces you to recognize what determines the objects of your science 'from the outside.' Over this you have no power. Your freedom from value judgments is as necessary as it is mere appearance. For neutrality is *real* only when it has the power of resisting interference. Otherwise it becomes the victim, as well as the aid, of every power that wants to use it." (Marcuse, "Industrialism and Capitalism," in *Negations*, p. 215.)

[20] *Natural Right and History*, p. 47.

Löwith, that understanding a world that has become challenging requires an acknowledgement of the need for challenging truths or heroic stances towards one's present—or the need to see objectivity as a heightened consciousness of subjectivity—the self-defeating character of Weber's nominalism, and therefore the doctrine of value-neutrality, appears obvious. The requirement of value neutrality requires the rational inquirer to view with indifference, at least for the purposes of observation, all attempts to justify the values that he or she does or might hold. Strauss therefore concludes that the search for truth would start from a standpoint which no one could find humanly compelling. It is at the very least paradoxical to claim that in order to understand how the important questions have or might be addressed, one must first dismiss the very possibility that these questions, as value questions, are susceptible to the search for truth. If we presuppose, as Weber ultimately must, that all truth is contextual, then this requires not only a self-denying attitude toward scientific rationality, but also an irrationalist metaphysics.

Strauss' thought itself seems to require that rational thought can only emerge from an engagement with important questions that transcend history, such as 'What is virtue?' or 'What is the good life for man?' Consequently he finds himself agreeing with Habermas (although through an entirely different route) that within any ultimate conception of reality guidance by the process of free questioning (which does not include a promise that a definitive answer to the questions will be found) can be shown to be intrinsically worthwhile.[21] Indeed Strauss does more than simply remind us that the kind of science to which Weber aspired could not consistently operate according to generalizable norms of thought. The paradox of Weber's views appears even if one accepts Jaspers contention that Weber's was an attempt to attune the task of conceptual understanding in science to responsibility for the "events and decisions" of the present with all of their unique complexities. In this vein Weber had to declare science to be a means of personally measuring up to the demands of a world which he had to accept as fate.

---

[21] For a comparative treatment of Habermas' and Strauss' contribution to the debate on Weber's thought see R. Factor and S. Turner, *Max Weber and the Debate over Reason and Value*, p. 208ff.

But then, as Strauss insists, it is an attitude toward fate, rather than an attribute of reason, which makes it rationally impossible to defend scientific objectivity itself as an autonomous value.[22] For Weber this simply required that the production of scientific findings should be kept independent of whether the inquirer or her addressee wants to promote one among the many conflicting choices that they themselves might face as actors (and which science tries to clarify for them).

Strauss contends that in the name of clarifying our cultural horizon Weberian social science undermines the original function of any genuinely critical knowledge of values, namely that it begins in taking seriously the "natural understanding," or the evaluating attitudes of human beings, in order to expose their possible shortcomings to themselves and thereby aim at perfecting themselves.[23] A pre-emptive rejection of the transition from non-evaluating objectivity to evaluative reason is at the very root of Weber's conception of objectivity. Weber never shows that values cannot be rationally criticized but rather assumes it, and goes on to develop a philosophy according to which there is no value system—no distinction between good and evil, the very things about which human beings actually struggle—whose claim to be true is *worth* rational examination. This is the case even though Weber insists that one continues and must continue, to believe in such distinctions.[24]

In most interpretations, Weber's work points either to a post-enlightenment conception of human autonomy or to an entirely inhuman ideal which presupposes that the foundations of human freedom could never be won by overcoming irrationality or the struggle for power. In sum Weber holds fast to the idea that the human situation is defined by struggle, and that the value of struggle itself can never be transcended by humanity's efforts to gain autonomous insight into these conflicts. But Strauss seems to believe that the encounter with Weber is most disturbing when one pushes his thought to be more consistent.[25] In this

---

[22] *Natural Right and History*, p. 73.

[23] Ibid., p. 79.

[24] These points inform Strauss' "Social Science and Humanism"; Cf. Castoriadis, *Philosophy, Politics and Autonomy*, p. 75.

[25] This point is made by R. Eden in "Why wasn't Weber a nihilist?" in *The Crisis*

regard, what is troubling in Weber is his implicit assumption that the defense of philosophy or science inevitably rests upon a "sacrifice of the intellect" and that therefore the search for truth itself is really a disclosure of our need for a tragic view of reality.

However, Strauss' commentary also intimates that Weber's ultimate ethical 'problem' was more pronounced in his strictly scientific work than previously suggested. Weber seemed to 'evaluate' cultures according to the chances for the development of human nobility within them. As we saw earlier, Wilhelm Hennis has suggested that this was Weber's permanent concern.[26] On the basis of an often-ignored passage in Weber's essay on value neutrality Hennis shows how all of Weber's sociological research was "oriented to the higher question of the *Typus Mensch* positively or negatively formed under the impact of [a given set of social power] relations." In modernity the chances of human nobility depend upon the rise to superiority of a type of person who could articulate or follow the demands of moral seriousness in secular life even though the means of secular freedom and rationalization had depreciated the need for moral seriousness. Although Weber did not want to use science to evaluate a world dominated by "specialists without spirit and sensualists without heart"[27] he nevertheless oriented science toward an exploration of the alternative possibilities of genuine leadership, socially creative domination and the will to provocation in the search for truth. Although Weber believed that as a scientist he could not legitimately use cultural or ethical standards as criteria for a rational understanding of society and history, he himself appeared to propose a quality of 'leadership' in culture and ethics as just such a criterion. This suggests, Strauss claims, that when Weber saw that the limits of reason stemmed from the requirement to justify its claims by value-neutral means, he was looking for an alternative way to establish commitment to higher standards.[28]

---

of *Liberal Democracy: A Straussian Perspective*, ed. K. Deutsche and W. Soffer.

[26] W. Hennis, *Max Weber: Essays in Reconstruction,* p. 152.

[27] Weber, *The Protestant Ethic*, p. 182.

[28] On the importance of this point to Strauss, as well as Aron's inability to refute it in a straightforward manner, see Tzevan Todorov, "Le Debat des valeurs: Weber—Strauss—Aron," p. 62.

According to Strauss, then, Weber had a definitive view of basic (in principle, transhistorical) human alternatives according to which the relation between reason and the requirements of moral seriousness in culture could be addressed. On the one hand, one could have recourse to this-worldly values, in which case one was fated to side with the success of rational capitalism and science. Alternatively, one could seek meaning in other-worldly values, in which case one would be relying on religion to meet the fundamental inner needs of man.[29] But Strauss then wonders why Weber explicitly disqualified religion as an adequate proving ground for the serious life. His answer is that Weber's watchword of intellectual integrity, his refusal to bring the sacrifice of the intellect, forces him to acknowledge the tie between thought and fate: "We are irreligious because fate forces us to be irreligious and for no other reason."[30] Consequently, if the modern world can become a proving ground for moral seriousness, there is no other choice but to cultivate this quality within the hard realism of politics or the openness to inconvenient facts demanded by science. But Weber also must have seen, according to Strauss, that the conflict between the claims of faith and the claims of free insight is *the* eternal conflict, that each can claim to correspond to the most important needs of human beings.

Indeed in "Science as a Vocation" Weber proclaimed that the dignity of a human life consists in either really bringing the "sacrifice of the intellect", and thereby seeing God as the ultimate power in every struggle, or facing up to the "demands of the day" without hope for prophetic illumination. Weber's work, however, is distinguished by his confession that he was fated-to follow the demands associated with the success of this-worldly reason. In this regard, Strauss suggests, it is fate, and not the power of autonomous insight itself, which determines how the conflict between science and religion, politics and ethical universalism, can be decided within the framework of Weber's thought.[31]

We can highlight Strauss' point here by pointing to a basic divergence between Weber's views on the ethico-political consequences

---

[29] *Natural Right and History*, p. 71.
[30] Ibid., p. 73.
[31] Ibid.

of value-conflict and the foundations of liberalism. Weber presumes that liberal tolerance or neutrality is no solution to the war of the gods. As Strauss argues, Weber ultimately had to structure his basic attitude toward reason around the idea that it was not possible for the genuinely modern social scientist or political actor to confront the implications of his or her own 'faith' while acknowledging the equal claims of all faiths.[32] Among other things, this accounts for why he believed that social scientific objectivity would be a curse if it actually led acting and choosing individuals to view reality, or the necessity of choice, from a value-neutral perspective. In this context he willingly admits that each faith *is* a choice between God and the Devil the substantive requirements of which are incompatible with those of other choices. Since it is not possible to respect the equal claims of all values under these conditions Weber is left only with the task of finding a higher, more life-affirming basis for becoming a choosing, evaluative being.[33]

Strauss insists that it is only on this basis that we get a glimpse of the way Weber could hope to evade the intellectual crisis within which his basic insights were entangled. The philosophical imperative to search for an "enhancement of man" in Nietzsche's sense forces Weber to interpret humanity's subjection to eternal conflict in a religious way even as he finds himself bound by the "demands of the day" to this-worldly meaning. From Strauss' point of view it is therefore impossible to defend Weber's underlying preference for 'vitalistic' values as a moral position at all.[34] By the time he wrote "Science as a Vocation" it was apparent to Weber that the actual choice to follow the god of science or autonomous insight could not be rationally defended but rather rests simply on an act of faith. This is why Weber's overt defense is related to forbearance of the demands of the day. But Strauss argues that Weber's claim that one is fated to believe, at least confirms his deep allegiance to the thesis of faith. In other words Weber's affirmation of science implies that our "yearning for a solution to the riddle of being" cannot be satisfied by the life of free investigation.[35]

---

[32] Weber, "The Meaning of 'Ethical Neutrality'," p. 18.
[33] *Natural Right and History*, p. 44.
[34] Ibid., p. 46.
[35] Ibid., p. 75.

This is why, according to Strauss, Weber affirms intellectual integrity rather than the power of the "knowable truth." But at the same time he was haunted by the suspicion that science itself rests on "the sacrifice of the intellect."

Robert Eden, who has extended Strauss' understanding of Weber, has argued that Weber could only sustain his "productive contradiction" (Löwith) between heroic individualism and this-worldly reason by seeking the moral high ground in an ungrounded choice to align oneself with the success of liberalism.[36] Weber does not believe in liberalism since he does not believe that value conflicts could be resolved by the principle of tolerance or abstract respect for persons, which requires neutrality toward cultural values or non-instrumental treatment of others. As we have seen earlier, Weber's politics would organize society around the imperative to breed personal excellence and resoluteness in the sphere of decision and responsibility. Accordingly, the highest ethical distinction itself must be beyond good and evil.[37] However compelling liberal morality is, it does not ensure the most compelling need of liberalism itself, namely that the choice to follow its demands will amount to a freely motivated choice for tolerance or non-instrumental treatment of others. One must still reckon with those who treat the consequences of liberalism as threatening to values that have motivating power only if there is a "knowable good." There is a sense, then, that liberalism cannot apply tolerance and neutrality to its own practices. Indeed it must be intolerant of those who would be guided by faith and prejudiced against those who believe in an objectively knowable good. We know, from many of today's moral controversies, that everything depends upon the extent to which the state is given power or responsibility to reject intolerant views or exclusive ways of life. Liberal morality cannot tell us whether the use of this power is more urgent or less urgent than the right to pursue one's ends freely however intolerant of alternatives they turn out to be.

Weber's answer to this situation is to argue for the priority of politics in dramatizing the "ultimate" problems of human striving itself. We must remember that the ethic of responsibility is not intended to

---

[36] R. Eden, *Political Leadership and Nihilism*, pp. 34–5.
[37] *Natural Right and History*, p. 46.

vitiate moral considerations. Rather it shows how the demands of moral reflection posed by the question of how to direct human beings toward their highest possibilities can only be genuinely raised in so far as one recognizes that the question is already political. Indeed, *contra* Kant, in a secular society the purely moral agent would have to justify her choice to avoid considerations about the contingencies of her action. Choosing beings are always already faced with a conflict between ultimate authorities among which is the conflict between success or rational moral principle. In politics one is accountable for accounting for one's actions morally. By the same token the genuine politician cannot avoid, through mere compromise, the tragic quality of political action—which means that she must know that considerations about the efficiency of the means, foreseeability of consequences and the intrinsic worthiness of the end are incommensurable.

For Weber the "genuine political leader" was the ultimate guarantor of that quality of action which derives from the knowledge of tragedy. Indeed Strauss shows that Weber did not really rely upon fate, *as opposed to* reason (the search for evident grounds for belief), to provide adequate insight into the alternative between autonomous insight and revelation, science and politics. Rather he plainly articulated the view that "man needs the necessity of guilt," or tragic moral choices, for true access to the highest human possibilities.

Strauss forces us to account for the disparity between, on the one hand, Weber's own scientific and political claims and aspirations, which involved a qualified, albeit pragmatic, support for both the liberal social order and the value of theoretical insight, and, on the other hand, the kind of nihilism implicit in his historicism and relativism.[38] Strauss therefore doubts whether it is possible to mitigate the nihilistic consequences of modern thought. His critique is clearly driven by the perception that social scientific objectivity, as Weber sees it, prevents one from understanding and confronting the crisis of modern society openly and directly. In order for Weber to elaborate a secular ethics and politics of serious culture, he must reject any attempt to re-animate liberal democracy which has simply become culturally successful. The

---

[38] This is Eden's key point in his *Political Leadership and Nihilism*.

important drive behind Weber's work was the search for a worthwhile, ennobling liberal democratic social order. But Weber clearly seemed most troubled by the fact that liberal democratic thought and practice appeared to privilege means of secular freedom and autonomy according to which human beings are not distinguished by their worthwhile or ennobling qualities.

MAKING POLITICS SAFE FOR PHILOSOPHY

Strauss devoted a considerable portion of his writings to historicists like Weber, and especially Nietzsche. The influence of these thinkers, he argues, compels us to deepen our understanding of the intellectual crisis in modern liberal democracies. Although in Weber's work there is some resonance of one of Strauss' leading themes—the Aristotelian question of the type of human being that should be produced by a society[39]—Weber nevertheless denied himself recourse to the transhistorical standards that would make this question meaningful in Strauss' terms. Consquently, he refused to be guided by the question of the "best regime," and instead turned to the alternative between creative struggle and pacifying routine.[40] As an historicist Weber suggested that the culture of liberal democracy (not its ideals) would have to be reconstructed from political life without Nietzsche's "pathos of distance."[41]

According to Strauss there is a kind of latent, unacknowledged critique of liberalism in modern social science. As we have seen the central paradox of social science lies in its presupposition that it is possible to treat one's own interest in asking certain questions as contingent. To take social science seriously we must be worried about the fate of our culture, or chosen cultural standpoint, without claiming to have good reasons to defend our values as more worthy of assent than others. Strauss considers it paradoxical that the goal of Weber's science was to attain a rational understanding of meaningful phenomena even as

---

[39] This interpretation is often found in Hennis, *Max Weber: Essays in Reconstruction.*

[40] *Natural Right and History*, pp. 49, 65; This theme is dealt with at greater length in other commentaries, perhaps especially in Wolfgang Mommsen, "Personal Conduct and Societal Change" in *Max Weber, Rationality and Modernity*, ed. S. Whimster and S. Lash.

[41] Weber, "National Character and the Junkers" in *From Max Weber*, p. 393.

that very model of rationality disqualified the concern with the truth or superiority of one's values as an independently important source of meaning. Strauss remarks, however, that Weber tried to distinguish his thought from historicism.[42] For Weber what is distinctive about the search for the truth is not that all truths are contextual, but that truth is merely one among a number of possible "elementary" cultural standpoints, and one who adopts the standpoint of this cultural sphere makes a subjective decision resting on faith, and must follow its intrinsic demands or else fail to live meaningfully. There are intrinsic demands within each ultimate value sphere and, since they are in conflict with one another, there are no independently important sources of meaning except the nobility with which one struggles for one's god or demon. According to Strauss this means that the truth is not a noble objective, but that the search for truth can be qualified as noble to the extent that one is following its demands out of a special kind of commitment rather than because the goal can be defended as necessary for living well.[43]

Strauss proposes that Weber's thought, and historicism in general, implies a rejection of the foundations of political philosophy. The main elements of Strauss' attempt to recover the original meaning of political philosophy are familiar. While he agrees with Weber that philosophy or science must be autonomous, he also argues that political philosophy must enter the marketplace and speak with citizens in their own terms. Political philosophy is really the "political treatment of philosophy" whereby the philosopher urges the best citizens to see that their responsibility depends upon knowledge of the good rather than upon treating their values as beyond question or as subject to mere consensus.[44] On the one hand, citizens do not, and cannot, love the truth for its own sake, since this implies that there is no higher value than questioning value beliefs. Political life, or any mode of solidarity, will require a foundation in certain absolute commitments to a view of human perfection *or* a foundation in the expedient of consensus. Of

---

[42] *Natural Right and History*, p. 37–9.

[43] Strauss, "What is Political Philosophy?," p. 19; *Natural Right and History*, pp. 46–7.

[44] Strauss, "On Classical Political Philosophy" in *What is Political Philosophy?*, pp. 93–4.

course even the best citizens are not naturally philosophical, but only naturally ripe for philosophy. They do not want their values to go untested since if all values were merely conventional, or if the belief in their legitimacy were simply the convenient result of socialization, then there would be nothing noble in trying to safeguard or exemplify the way of life prescribed by their ordering of values.[45] Because it is natural in political life to distinguish between higher and lower, between the responsibility for a choiceworthy way of life and the mere concern for power or self-preservation, philosophers can at least get the best citizens interested in asking about what is intrinsically good.

In the light of these considerations Strauss claims that philosophers and citizens find different sources of meaning independently important. Philosophers are happy only with a life of free inquiry, an activity whose goals are necessarily independent of those of politics and unaffected by conventional objects of desire. For this reason the philosopher does not simply share with the best citizens a non-utilitarian conception of the good, but also knows that what is genuinely good can only be found beyond society. The philosopher is both responsible and truly happy, according to Strauss, only in the company of those with whom he can be socially irresponsible.[46] For citizens, however, the independently important sources of meaning are either the defense of certain values in conflict with those defended by other cities, or the defense of the city for its own sake. In the case of the latter—that is, patriotism—the preservation of the city is all that matters. For the partisan, however, political life involves achieving a way of life that recognizes certain values as better than others. To this extent, the object of political responsibility is not a society's self-interest, but its "public morality." One cannot adopt a public morality if it is said to rest solely on commitment, but only if it rests on a belief in a way of

---

[45] This is a distillation of Strauss' argument first offered in the chapter entitled "Classical Natural Right" in *Natural Right and History*, pp. 120–153. One finds it developed with a great deal of interpretive ingenuity by many Straussian scholars and especially in Strauss' famous and controversial reading of Plato's *Republic* in *The City and Man*, ch. 2.

[46] Strauss, "Liberal Education and Responsibility" in *Introduction to Political Philosophy*, p. 329.

life that recognizes intrinsically choiceworthy ends. Political philosophers, Strauss says, will be partisans of a certain type.[47]

But Strauss argues that political philosophy is based on the recognition that a rational approach to political controversies can only end in discussions about the nature of the "complete" good which lies beyond politics; and in this respect citizens and philosophers cannot be in complete agreement. This reveals why classical natural right was aristocratic: only an aristocratic class could harmonize the pursuit of political justice with the desire to gain appreciation of intrinsically choiceworthy ends. The philosophers, who know that the highest good is only available through their private erotic activity of challenging convention, adapted what they said in their writings to the prudent goal of supporting those who can be viewed not only as the best candidates to rule the city but also those who might best tolerate the anti-social proclivities of philosophers. For this reason books like Plato's *Republic* could be exoterically designed around the teaching that the education of a natural aristocracy to true virtue was, in its most essential aspect, a preparation for ruling the city. But the real teaching was that the philosophers, the real experts in true virtue, could not return to the cave of public affairs except as a "necessary evil."[48]

Strauss implies that, from the standpoint of political philosophy, any regime can be prudentially justifiable depending upon the historical and social circumstances of philosophy.[49] Esoteric writing will always be necessary since the true interest of the naturally best way of life (that of the philosopher) is not to serve society, and the citizens cannot really accept the anti-social nature of the philosopher's true desires. What is interesting about the philosophical founders of liberal democratic politics is not so much their normative position but the fact that they found their own kind of prudence.[50] They defined public morality only in terms of limiting the purposes of political life and lowering the standards to

---

[47] *The City and Man*, p. 47

[48] Ibid., p. 83.

[49] This has caused Bernard Susser to remark that Strauss' thought is really a kind of "sociology of truth." (Susser, "Leo Strauss: The Ancient as Modern," p. 503).

[50] The following abbreviated account of Strauss' argument may be gleaned from "What is Political Philosophy?" pp. 40–55 and "The Three Waves of Modernity" in *Introduction to Political Philosophy*.

which the striving of individuals must conform in a just society with a workable public morality. This made possible a more realistic appeal to the utilitarian selfishness of individuals. If human beings are intrinsically selfish then at least they can be relied upon to obey an order which requires them only to agree upon the less demanding interest they all equally share, prosperous security or unencumbered selfhood. There is no need to discriminate among high and low if freedom can be a universal right, limited only by one's capacity for enlightened self-interest, rather than a privilege of the lucky or naturally favoured few. The material conditions for comfort and access to education are sufficiently available to all, due at least in part to the influence of philosophy and science, so that an expedient order can be fashioned on the basis of everyone's capacity to look out for herself.

But this very same world of liberal democracy eventually became the home of historicizing social science as well. This has meant that liberals have become educated to believe that all commitments that underlie one's attachment to the goals of one's society, group or private desire are equal. Again, what is of interest is the difference between early modernity and late modernity. The goal of openness in society had originally been considered good because individuals were thereby protected from non-universalistic treatment based on contingent access to unequal power or talent, and from the idea that morality requires unquestioned authority. Now openness is considered good because it has been found to be impossible to discriminate among ultimately subjective ends or conceptions of happiness or because it treats all people as capable of developing their own conception of happiness for themselves.[51] Social science completes the late-modern conception by proposing that it is impossible to resolve the question of the validity of values rationally. That is, not only does it reject the classical view that human life can be characterized by intrinsically choiceworthy ends, but its conception of intellectual integrity pulls the rug from under our belief in the possibility that the liberal social order will afford progress in moral matters as well. The separation between the public and the private in Lockean liberalism seemed to presuppose that the

---

[51] *The City and Man*, pp. 31–32.

independence of the individual was the moral condition for the exercise of freedom. But the fulfilment of this precondition cannot be legally guaranteed since it requires the counterpart notion of "moral education" which has been rejected in contemporary liberalism.[52] Once the sovereignty of the people is recognized as the principle of political legitimacy it becomes increasingly absurd to speak of liberal democracy as a form of rule conditioned by virtue or natural law, and therefore absurd to hold the sovereign responsible for itself.[53] Strauss' story of political philosophy since Rousseau ends with the dominance of historicist social science. This doctrine proposes firstly, that all moralities are merely conventionally necessary elements of solidarity; and secondly that since moral controversy resolves itself into the conflict of ultimate values the basis of politically legitimate rule must therefore be defined apart from it.

With the open declaration of the pseudo-naturalness of every public morality the most influential thinkers accept the historicist thesis that the nature of humanity is indeterminate and that every culture is a result of a creative ordering of otherwise blind forces or potentials. Rousseau remained only a proto-historicist since he still "saw clearly the disproportion between...undefined and undefinable freedom and the requirements of civil society."[54] The concepts of history and culture which followed, however, entailed a process that cannot be rationally or objectively evaluated by any standards outside of itself. Those heroic individuals who can live with the insight into the contingent character of all truths—including that of the interpretation of life as will to power which follows from this insight—must at least acknowledge that every "view of the whole" implies a horizon with no other support but itself.[55]

Hence the standard that supplants nature, and even history, is that of authenticity, which occasions Nietzsche's "creative call to creativity."[56] The only alternative left for the philosopher is either to

---

[52] Strauss, "Political Philosophy and the Crisis of our Time" in *The Post-Behavioural Era*, p. 222.

[53] Ibid.; Cf. Rousseau, *The Social Contract*, Bk I, Ch. VII.

[54] *Natural Right and History*, p. 294.

[55] Ibid., p. 27.

[56] Strauss, *Studies in Platonic Political Philosophy*, p. 186; *What is Political Philosophy?*, p. 54.

live for the emergence of an "enhanced humanity" and therefore view politics itself as an experimental context for philosopher-artists or to free everyone from responsibility and provide no political or cultural limits that would prevent them from pursuing happiness in a way that is indifferent to its value for human development.[57] Nietzsche's call to make oneself into a new context for human development made responsibility impossible in practice. Strauss believes that the only hope in the modern situation is that this "theoretical crisis" might not be an irretrievably practical one.[58] But for this he relied upon the existence of enemies or other non-rational factors of socialization which would inspire a faith among liberal democrats in the purposes of their country.

For Strauss of course, the philosopher will, by writing esoterically, support the regime in power, or the regime from whose power he can most benefit. He does this so as to preserve a space for those aspects of philosophy that are not socially responsible in the normal sense. Bloom suggests that the philosophic founders of liberal democracy gave the people what they wanted in order to be given an officially recognized right to pursue an activity in which they would be bound to be misunderstood by them.[59] In terms of the goals of his writings, Strauss' adoption of a politically and culturally elitist rhetoric within the context of liberal democracy, and perhaps even his rejection of historicism, was not as deep as his commitment to preserve the radicalism of philosophy. For Strauss philosophy is the end for which politics is the means even though he develops this idea in contradistinction to Nietzsche's thought which implies "irresponsible indifference to politics." Unfortunately, from the standpoint of his own rationale for esotericism, one often doubts whether his political ideas are to be taken seriously at all except as an expedient for the practice of philosophy as he understands it. In the next chapter we will therefore discuss Richard Rorty's attempt to conceive of, and justify, a post-philosophical liberalism. According to

---

[57] Ibid., p. 55.

[58] "The Three Waves of Modernity", p. 98; "Progress or Return?", *Introduction to Political Philosophy*, p. 310. See also John G. Gunnell, "Political Theory and Politics: The case of Leo Strauss and Liberal Democracy" in *The Crisis of Liberal Democracy*, p. 86.

[59] Bloom, *The Closing of the American Mind*, p. 288-89.

Rorty, historicism need not produce either an intellectual culture which favours nihilism or a defense of liberalism which must shield the public from "dangerous truths."

Chapter Six

RORTY'S END OF PHILOSOPHY:
A NEW BEGINNING FOR LIBERALISM?

We have seen how some recent thinkers have sought to contest or amplify Weber's (and Nietzsche's) pessimism about moral-evaluative thought and practices in the modern world. The interpretation of Weber's work has been a kind of common touchstone for those who would draw radically different conclusions about the horizons of the liberal social order as well as the direction of political theory. Critics and defenders of liberalism alike can point to the Weberian view of modernity and show that the form in which liberal democracy has triumphed in the social world he described has led to morally ambiguous attitudes toward modern political life. The defenders often draw attention to features of liberalism that Weber either marginalizes or rejects, namely, its claims to cultural openness and its promise of progress, innovation, non-arbitrary authority (i.e. rational meritocracy) and autonomy as well as the possibility of a non-ideological ordering of social and political priorities and arrangements. Some, however, have questioned whether the political and cultural effects of rationalization can be described simply in terms of the so-called 'objective' functional requirements of a modernized society. Today, even the question of how best to account for the achievements or cultural success of liberal democracy has become as difficult and pressing for political thinkers in the era of the "end of ideology" as it was when the problems were said to lie within the field of ideological conflict itself.

But this is also because within the critical traditions of the social sciences and humanities today many of the strongest voices belong to those who challenge the philosophical defense of liberal democracy and its impact upon contemporary political culture. Writers like Bloom on the right, MacIntyre and other communitarians, and Foucault and Derrida on the cultural left, have significantly shaped the contours of contemporary discussion. Some, like Strauss and his followers, have purveyed a cultural conservatism which more or less blames indiscreet liberal openness and tolerance for the sins of relativism and nihilism in culture and philosophy. More recently, 'communitarian' thinkers have laid the blame on the 'thin' foundations of liberal public morality and have indicted liberalism for its inherent tilt toward utilitarian culture and for imposing a dehumanizing subjectivization of politics and culture which, in the name of Enlightenment, condones amoral interpretations of freedom, human striving, the sources of social solidarity and the moral purposes of political institutions. In this chapter we will discuss the recent work of Richard Rorty who argues that we can have a liberalism that dignifies moral attachments even while it promotes the disenchantment of the world in all the above-mentioned respects. Following John Dewey's pragmatism, Rorty argues that the crisis of liberal culture is related to our adherence to an obsolete intellectual paradigm which obscures the possibilities for reconstructing liberalism's cultural and moral claims in a post-metaphysical age. Rorty's book, *Contingency, Irony and Solidarity*, seeks to attract contemporary intellectuals to the belief that they can recover—perhaps for the first time—the creativity and vitality of liberal culture only by casting aside the metaphysical baggage of both its philosophical critics and defenders.

BEYOND INTELLECTUAL CRISIS

At least since Rousseau many have contended that the Enlightenment founders of liberalism established an all-too-convenient account of how social and political arrangements could be brought into harmony with the security and self-formation of free individuals. The staunchest critics of liberalism usually challenge its implicit conception of "negative" freedom and "unencumbered" selfhood. Rarely, however, do critics of Enlightenment liberalism directly disparage the historical project of institutionalizing individual freedoms and the need to shed the yoke of parochialism, sectarianism and dogmatic authority. They are more concerned about the development of an individualist-utilitarian conception of the self in which exclusive focus is placed on the capacity to choose one's own conception of the good and attachments. Enlightenment utilitarianism is said to disqualify more positive accounts of the constitutive goods of self-realization, and of a common order realized through the flourishing of direct, communal attachments in favor of the rational egoism of citizens.[1]

For Rorty, the problem runs deeper than what is suggested in the contemporary debate between liberals and communitarians. As we have seen, for Strauss the development of an intellectual culture prepared to celebrate openly the pseudo-naturalness of every public morality could only become a breeding ground for nihilism whether it favored such a result or not. Rorty believes that the debate among liberals and communitarians comes down to these fears about the role of the philosopher. He insists, however, that liberals who are historicists and nominalists can assume meaningful responsibility for their liberal moral and political beliefs and their consequences. In support of Rorty one can argue that neither Strauss nor MacIntyre can offer an independent defense of the natural rights perspective or communitarian justice. In the case of MacIntyre, he restricts himself to accounts about what kinds of people and action-orientations would become exemplary in a society in which the natural rights perspective was adopted, and which negative, superficial or manipulative character types have come to proliferate in a society which denies the validity of that perspective. As for Strauss, he offers no rational argument against the view of Nietzsche that the real struggle is between life-affirming and decadent values, except to suggest that this is an indecent way of defining the problem of politics which exposes the fact that philosophy deals with dangerous truths.[2]

Strauss argued that political philosophy must at least publicly promote conceptions of virtue, or conceptions of human development that are founded on the universal meaning of human striving. What Rorty finds conspicuous here is that philosophers have played a large

---

[1] See especially Charles Taylor, *Hegel*. Cambridge: Cambridge University Press, 1975.

[2] Rorty, "The Priority of Democracy to Philosophy" in *Objectivity Relativism and Truth*, p. 194 and "Straussianism, Democracy and Allan Bloom."

part in the development of liberal culture, not because of the influence of their "ideas," but largely because of the influence of the very ethos of philosophy. In this respect, Rorty claims that what needs to be criticized in political philosophy is precisely the *role* the philosopher has played in relating justice to the perfection or transparency of human striving. What is important for philosophical liberalism is that the search for the real good for individual human beings can be regarded as convergent with a sense of justice.[3]

Today, according to Rorty, historicism and 'post-modern' philosophy have cast doubt on this attempt to place the search for ourselves and our accountability to others "in a single vision." Most importantly, the Romantic-historicist tradition has caused us to view the search for the self as a matter of idiosyncratic self-creation. But according to Rorty a new historicist intellectual culture would reach beyond the horizon not only of traditional philosophy but also beyond Nietzschean scepticism (or, more broadly, European moral scepticism) as well. On the one hand, we would have to stop describing the relation between our private selves and our public attachments by a unifying purpose lying beyond them, such as the recognition of the real or primary goods for human beings. On the other hand, we should not go over to the side of the sceptics and their claim that "there is *no* sense of human solidarity, that this sense is a mere artifact of human socialization."[4]

According to Rorty one can say that historicism has demonstrated the limits of the Enlightenment temptation to make human nature more transparent to itself. Instead it began to place the accent upon enlarging our "vocabularies of moral reflection."[5] Philosophy began to enter the discursive universe of the poets and revolutionaries who "have sensed not that an enduring, substratal human nature has been suppressed or repressed by 'unnatural' or 'irrational' social institutions but rather that changing languages and other social practices may produce human beings of a sort that had never before existed."[6]

---

[3] Rorty, *Contingency, Irony and Solidarity*, p. xiii.
[4] Ibid., pp. xiv, xiii.
[5] Rorty, "Freud and Moral Reflection," *Essays on Heidegger and Others*, p. 154–55.
[6] *Contingency, Irony and Solidarity*, p. 7.

We can supplement Rorty's account here by noting how the historicist-Romantic turn in philosophy has caused the alternative between historicism and evolutionism to appear. Historicism, as we have seen, can be said to have no way of resolving the tension between objectivity and commitment when it comes to trying to account rationally for the content of given patterns of socialization and culture. On the heels of the Kantian transformation of Enlightenment thought, the search for rational social arrangements became central to the *culture* of freedom. This is the only side of the Enlightenment that Rorty wants to retain. Liberalism was not only to be developed as a philosophical theme but also availed itself of new socio-historical self-descriptions as well. With very few qualifications Rorty places himself within the orbit of this late modern conception inaugurated by Romanticism and Hegel.[7] From Rousseau to Hegel philosophy itself came to acknowledge that the claims of reason cannot be ontologically separated from the cultural and historical self-determination of human powers. Indeed they suggested that reason is more like the result of a successful, self-conditioned process of socialization than the discovery of a natural starting point for the attainment of truth. For political philosophy itself it marked the abandonment of the idea that it is possible to speak of a 'natural' basis of freedom in society, such as the rational individual liberated from prejudice and tradition. Now the focus is placed on the dynamic potential of modern culture itself.

But Rorty laments that these developments were still conceived by the philosophers as moving us closer to the possession of a privileged "vocabulary" which would be best adapted to understanding the true nature of reality or human possibilities.[8] It can be noted that Rorty himself does not acknowledge that there was another alternative to historicism—namely, social evolutionism. For its part evolutionism simply broadens the concept of a rational society, replacing the theory of the natural progressiveness of post-traditional society with a model of the adaptive superiority or selection advantages provided by the cultural primacy of certain key institutions, social classes or personality types in modernity. However, there is a basic indecision within evolutionism as

---

[7] Ibid., pp. 6–8, 24–5.
[8] Ibid., p. 6.

to whether rationalization applies most to modern society's capacity to adapt to change and novelty through markets and instrumental rationality (as F. Hayek might suggest), or whether it applies to society's capacity to develop institutions that foster a cooperative mode of human solidarity. Evolutionism remains fertile ground, particularly for philosophers who know that many of their insights will depend upon the work of social theorists. This is especially true for those, like Habermas, who rightly emphasize the socially imposed deformations of the modern life-world by the reigning adaptive and socializing mechanisms. His is an attempt, combining Marx, Durkheim and Dewey, to overcome the abstract ties and alienated social relationships introduced by the one-sided dominance within liberal modernity of bureaucratic capitalism which has suppressed the authentic possibilities of democratic socialization.

Rorty does not place much faith in Habermas' critical theory of society, however. Rather he views Habermas as a representative of the contemporary rejection of historicism. He sides with Habermas' critique of Nietzschean post-enlightenment thought which undermines all possible claims of reason in favor of questions that must be decided in terms of the struggle for domination. But Habermas, like Strauss, fears that historicism has led to Nietzsche's view that every culture is an epiphenomenon of a process of non-rational unconscious adaptation. In Nietzsche historicism is radicalized by calling for the groundless affirmation of creativity in order to will a new context of human development. Habermas has stated that for Nietzsche the ultimate meaning of human development can only be decided by a process in which "one will responds to another; one force takes hold of another."[9] According to Rorty the mistake of both the philosophical left and the philosophical right has been their attempt to define our rational potential, or even our inevitable irrationality in matters of belief, as characterizing our underlying depth and universal nature.

---

[9] Habermas, *The Philosophical Discourse of Modernity*, p. 124; Despite his criticisms of Habermas on other issues, Rorty appears sufficiently comfortable with this characterization and critique of Nietzsche. He proposes that Nietzsche's own "substitution of self-creation for discovery" implies a predatory image of humankind. (*Contingency, Irony and Solidarity*, p. 20.)

According to Rorty, the best way to answer this tradition is to think of liberal democracy as prior to philosophy. Liberal democracy stands for the realization of a community of individuals culturally free to choose and reflectively define their own responsibilities and commitments without harming others. He is therefore prepared to endorse Mill's model of liberalism—albeit only on functional grounds, not as a version based on a truer account of reality or social needs. In fact the only kind of truth that should matter to historicists and nominalists is the kind of truth there can be in a liberal democracy; namely, whatever emerges from our open and experimental encounters with ourselves, our conversational partners and our social environments. The pragmatic reconstruction of liberalism implies: "if we take care of political and cultural freedom, truth and rationality will take care of themselves."[10]

In Rorty's and Dewey's pragmatic philosophy it is tempting to say that the notion of truth is abandoned altogether. But Rorty insists that all that he abandons is an orientation to truth that is expected to transcend contingency and specifiable means-ends relationships. He claims that his aim is to cure us of the need, bred into us by metaphysics, to transcend partisanship for a particular kind of community toward a partisanship for objectivity as such. In this connection he proposes that philosophical anxiety about relativism is a red herring.[11] Against the idea that truth is a result of sorting out the autonomous from the contingent, Rorty offers the nominalist suggestion that truth not be tied to the triumph of time and chance, that it be as flexible as any other technique we use for "altering ourselves and our environment to suit our aspirations."[12]

The philosophical genealogy of Rorty's new intellectual culture can be found in the anti-essentialist theories of language and meaning of Quine, Wittgenstein and Davidson, the post-modernism of Foucault and Derrida, and the re-appraisal of the cultural value of truth in Nietzsche, Freud and Dewey. All of these thinkers abandon the idea that human

---

[10] "Truth and Freedom: A Reply to Thomas McCarthy," p. 634.

[11] See especially "Solidarity and Objectivity" in Rorty, *Objectivism, Relativism and Truth*, p. 30 where Rorty characterizes relativism as a "red herring."

[12] "Texts and Lumps" in *Objectivism Relativism and Truth*, p. 81.

understanding can only be authoritative if it is related to something lying beyond our contingent beliefs and desires. Truth does not consist in the non-contingent beliefs we can or would need to have about those objects that are causally independent of our beliefs and desires. We should not speak of objects as something about which we can have justified beliefs, but rather as things that behave in such a way that "our practices will react to them with pre-programmed changes of belief."[13] Our failure to see this has led to the distinction between kinds of inquiry (natural sciences) that deal with objects against which our beliefs can be tested, and those kinds (cultural sciences) that deal with objects that force us to test our beliefs against other beliefs. Rorty argues that philosophy should see different types of inquiry as experiments, "designed to see if we can get what we want at a certain historical moment by using a certain language."[14]

This view of the replacement of philosophy by a linguistic meta-philosophy also exemplifies Rorty's approach to liberalism and political thought. Rorty claims that it is a mistake to believe that an appeal to truth can ever settle normative questions since we will always have a different conception of truth depending upon which contingent conception of human development we are trying to align ourselves with. When we engage in discussions about which values to promote, the appeal to "good arguments" is always a form of "obedience to our own conventions."[15] Rorty is concerned to evade the objections of philosophers like Habermas who say that his position is a form of self-defeating relativism, that he is merely presupposing what he is unable to show rationally—namely, the truth of the assertion that "obedience to our own conventions" is a worthy convention.

The pragmatist liberal vision would itself draw its strength from the historicist and nominalist claim that all communities and selves need to identify themselves with nothing more than contingent "re-weavings" of our desires and beliefs. Faced with this characterization intellectuals have merely to draw a simple normative lesson, namely, that they should learn to live with the "new fuzziness" that results when one can

---

[13] Ibid., p. 83.
[14] Ibid., p. 91.
[15] Rorty, *The Consequences of Pragmatism,* p. xlii.

no longer think of truth as something that is discovered, and when one stops thinking of the highest intellectual achievements as those which realize our potential to arrive at universal criteria.   In particular, intellectuals should realize that what they do best is to try out new vocabularies and to challenge themselves and others to find them useful (or not) for their private experiments in self-creation.   The new liberal intellectual would combine an appreciation of the public convenience of liberal political neutrality with the non-neutral aims supported by liberal solidarity, which demand that we try to avoid cruelty and the humiliation of others.   A liberal intellectual is one who, almost by instinct, tries to increase the opportunity for different kinds of people to be understood in their own terms.   In a pragmatist liberal order one would not ask the most important intellectuals—literary writers or journalists—to alleviate suffering or to justify a particular conception of freedom or equality.   Rather one would want them to invent a new vocabulary for highlighting or distinguishing the varieties of suffering or for finding new and better terms with which to discuss the meaning and requirements of freedom and equality.

THE PRAGMATIC RECONSTRUCTION
OF LIBERALISM

Rorty often defends his views on no other basis than a recognition of the type of society in which we live.   Ours is a society which has increasingly encouraged us to recognize that the terms which we use to justify our "actions, beliefs and lives" are contingent.   According to Rorty those who go on to have doubts about the adequacy of those terms, or the "final vocabulary" into which they have been socialized, are ironists.[16]   In this sense the ironist is rather like Strauss' philosopher.   But unlike Strauss, Rorty thinks most of us can live well enough simply as nominalists and historicists.   Nevertheless the life of the ironist intellectual is his main theme.   The ironist has a special ability to understand how the moral goals of freedom and equality, for instance, can be re-described to mean almost anything simply by shifting the terms we use to make our commitment to them attractive.   As Rorty

---

[16] *Contingency, Irony and Solidarity*, p. 73.

points out, the posture of the ironist is what allowed Michel Foucault to 're-describe' the supposedly progressive aspects of modern liberal societies as a replacement of older strategies of power, dealing with the state's relation to its subjects or the Pastor's relation to his flock, by different and more subtle strategies of power applied to the improvement or reform of individuality. Rorty argues that we should not see solidarity itself as a mere epiphenomenon of successful strategies of power, even though we should share Foucault's nominalism and recognize the contingent nature of the terms in which we justify our commitment to moral goals.[17]

Yet it often seems as if there is no real difference between the pragmatic reconstruction of liberal solidarity and the more "dangerous" view Rorty believes is held by most post-modern theorists like Foucault. Each side claims that the terms we use to talk about our moral goals are non-neutral, that they exist to "make certain things look good and other things look bad." As Rorty says, we have no better criterion for deciding whether or not our "final vocabulary" is desirable than whether it proves suitable for someone using it to tell the story of the good things in his or her life through it. But here Rorty makes an important distinction which he uses to justify his entire enterprise. Our moral goals need not be "re-described" from the start as arbitrary products of history, but as goals "our" kind of community refers to when we try to enable better and richer discussions about pressing moral, political or social problems. He claims that this allows for a certain re-description of liberalism itself.

> I want to see freely arrived at agreement as agreement on how to accomplish common purposes...but I want to see these common purposes against the background of an increasing sense of the radical diversity of private purposes, of the radically poetic character of individual lives, and of the merely poetic foundations of the "we-consciousness" which lies behind our social institutions.[18]

Only when we try to go beyond our 'desire for solidarity' and ask

---

[17] For Rorty's remarks on Foucault in his later work see *Contingency, Irony and Solidarity*, pp. 61–2 and "Moral Identity and Private Autonomy: The Case of Foucault" in *Essays on Heidegger and Others*.

[18] *Contingency, Irony and Solidarity*, p. 67.

whether we have arrived at an understanding of something "essential," or whether we have an objective understanding of the nature of social reality itself, do we raise the spectre of relativism and worry that we have failed to get at something more true than our own contingent process of socialization.[19]

Of course, Rorty believes that the most important precursor to his new liberal intellectual culture is to be found in the pragmatist philosophy of John Dewey. Indeed the leading purpose of Dewey's work was to show why it is futile to let the desire for objectivity take priority over the desire for solidarity. Pragmatists recommend a minimalist view of truth in accord with William James' statement that truth itself is merely useful belief.[20] Dewey himself believed that philosophers resisted pragmatism because it appeared to reduce criteria of truth and moral validity to whatever guarantees emotionally desirable results.[21] But Dewey argued that traditional philosophy saw rational endeavour as a way of speaking about or controlling experience which could prove its value only with reference to a kind of intelligence that transcends given means/ends relationships. According to Dewey, however, there is no source of intelligent judgement outside of experience and the creative or experimental ways of controlling it or responding to it. He therefore claimed that value-judgements are neither wholly subjective nor independent of experience: *"Judgements about values are judgements about the conditions and the results of experienced objects; judgements about that which should regulate the formation of our desires, affections and enjoyments."*[22]

Like Nietzsche, pragmatism looks at truth as merely a particular way of responding to contingency, one that has value only for reminding us how, and for what purposes, we have decided to anchor our instrumental ability to project into the future. Unlike Nietzsche, however, pragmatists do not diagnose the "will to truth" as a form of will to power. They do not claim that only those who assert themselves

---

[19] Ibid., pp. 92–93.
[20] "Solidarity or Objectivity," p. 22.
[21] John Dewey, "The Need for a Recovery of Philosophy," in *The Philosophy of John Dewey*, ed. J. McDermott, p. 92.
[22] From *The Quest For Certainty* in *The Philosophy of John Dewey*, p. 583.

through a 'higher' instrumental ability should rule. Although for pragmatists truth is not to be found in a method for dealing with the problems of our experience that lies beyond the influence of power, neither is it to be made subject to a privileged reinterpretation of nature. Rather it is only as valuable as the symbols a community possesses to discuss which consequences of social action are in need of control and further experiment.

Dewey's pragmatism of course bears the traces of historicist thought in rather fundamental ways. From the following quote it appears that Dewey's view of scientific progress very much echoes the historicist position of Thomas Kuhn:

> Old ideas give way slowly; for they are more than abstract logical forms and categories. They are habits, predispositions, deeply ingrained attitudes of aversion and preference. Moreover, the conviction persists—though history shows it to be a hallucination—that all the questions that the human mind has asked are questions that can be answered in terms of the alternatives that the questions themselves present. But in fact intellectual progress usually occurs through sheer abandonment of questions together with both of the alternatives they assume—an abandonment that results from their decreasing vitality and a change of urgent interest. We do not solve them: we get over them. Old questions are solved by disappearing, evaporating, while new questions corresponding to the changed attitude of endeavour and preference take their place.[23]

Pragmatism is therefore reviled for recommending that philosophy become a handmaiden of one's empirically given society and its self-satisfied striving to make its values successful. Even Dewey, when he is contesting the separation of theory and practice, tends to give this impression:

> Men readily persuade themselves that they are devoted to intellectual certainty for its own sake. Actually they want it because of its bearing on safeguarding what they desire and esteem. The need for protection and prosperity in action created the need for warranting the validity of intellectual beliefs.[24]

---

[23] Dewey, *The Influence of Darwin on Philosophy: And other Essays on Contemporary Thought*, p. 19.
[24] From *The Quest For Certainty*, reprinted in *The Philosophy of John Dewey*, p.

In order to mitigate the utilitarian connotations of pragmatic method Dewey wanted to show how science and philosophy, pragmatically understood, could themselves be seen as models of public intelligence. Weber, who strove to eliminate utilitarian connotations from his approach, would seem to have simply pre-empted public intelligence, citing the irreconcilable pluralism of value-spheres and the necessary gap between clarifying ultimate value-standpoints and acting upon them.

Weber's view of disenchantment implied a tragic view of the crises brought about by the modern differentiation between the aims of science and those of evaluative life. For Dewey this same phenomenon came to mean that science is no longer to be praised as the pursuit of "pure knowledge" but as a way of becoming aware of and solving problems in a new way, that is, by making possible more practically intelligent aspirations in the realm of values. Both Dewey and Rorty suggest that the most promising 'symbol' conferred by science in a liberal democracy would not be the discovery of truth but the liberal priority of persuasion over force that gives our society the responsiveness to change that we want from it. According to Rorty, pragmatism, like Romanticism before it, shifts our attention away from the metaphor of discovering truth toward the metaphor of making truth.

It is well-known that by focusing on the control of experience Dewey usually espoused a scientistic view of the conditions of freedom and the realization of the good society. Therefore, in his social philosophy the idea of liberal democracy lay in its affinity to the practices of science. As Dewey put it, a "democratically organized public" is not itself a scientific community but it nevertheless requires "freedom of social inquiry and of distribution of its conclusions" much like the latter.[25] For Dewey truth is 'made' by a process of public communication that is functioning well, for otherwise scientific truth is merely what gets communicated as the results of discovery that is not yet fully combined with experiment. Free communication as it applies to science is not freedom to use an instrument after it has been fashioned, rather it implies effective public access to the process of inquiry thereby allowing the formation of new plans, instruments and

---

381.
[25] Dewey, *The Public and its Problems*, p. 166.

experiments to be regulated by a more dynamic access to the meaning of their possible consequences.[26] Since the experimental process can not simply be confined to the laboratory, the relation of science to democracy is not simply the requirement to place technical expertise in the service of the satisfaction of pre-given public goals. On the contrary, the success of the experimental process depends in large measure upon a well-formed public functioning as a feedback mechanism used to identify and aid in discovering the consequences to be controlled.[27] Dewey even goes so far as to say that without the participation of a well-formed public, science would not be worthy of the name.

According to Rorty, pragmatism re-defines the scientific calling as a "responsibility to human power." He would characterize Weber's requirement to separate facts from values as a legacy of philosophy's attempt to become responsible to transcendent powers.[28] Weber believed that the separation of facts from values is necessary if one wants to follow and preserve the inner integrity of thought in a culture that externally reduces thought either to a means to an end or to a mode of personal expression. He insisted that, internally, science could "serve moral forces" by determining where the commitment to clarifying ultimate meanings ends and mere wishful thinking begins. What became paramount to him was the chance that science could transcend its own positivism by attracting personalities who could find higher meaning in the secularized vocational service to the internal values of science.

But for Rorty such a view still bears the mark of an attempt to occupy a high ground, beyond good and evil as it were, from which nihilism, relativism and the subjectivization of values can be overcome. He argues that it was the mistake of thinkers like Nietzsche and Foucault to try to find a substitute for objectivity and the ethical

---

[26] For a similar conception of inquiry see Charles Lindblom, *Inquiry and Change: The Troubled Attempt to Understand and Shape Society.*

[27] For a similar view see Carole Pateman, *Participation and Democratic Theory*, p. 43.

[28] In Rorty's view we must do away with the model of the scientist who "selflessly expresses himself again and again to the hardness of facts." ("Science as Solidarity" in *Objectivism, Relativism and Truth*, p. 35.)

neutralization of personality in a world that makes us more subject to "instrumental rationality." Pragmatism, by contrast, would finally afford the opportunity to replace the "desire for objectivity" with the "desire for solidarity."

> Pragmatism seems to me...a philosophy of solidarity rather than of despair...[T]he pragmatist suggestion that we substitute a "merely" ethical foundation for our sense of community—or, better, that we think of our sense of community as having no foundation except shared hope and the trust created by such sharing—is put forward on practical grounds. It is *not* put forward as a corollary of a metaphysical claim that the objects in the world contain no intrinsically action-guiding properties, nor of an epistemological claim that we lack a faculty of moral sense, nor of a semantical claim that truth is reducible to justification. It is a suggestion about how we might think of ourselves in order to avoid the kind of resentful belatedness—characteristic of the bad side of Nietzsche—which now characterizes much of high culture. This resentment arises from the realization...that the Enlightenment's search for objectivity has often gone sour.[29]

Pragmatism therefore provides a way of "redescribing" institutions like science as being progressive only in those qualities they share with art and poetry.[30] We would still want the identity of science to be tied to the search for objectivity only if we still thought it was necessary to ask whether or not our way of using language to "carve up the world" corresponds to reality itself. However, our historicism has taught us that when we consider the merits of competing truths, beliefs or values we should not hope to discover anything more primary about ourselves or our world than whether or not the contingent "final vocabulary" we use still serves us or not. Judgements about this are not arbitrary, but depend only on finding another more attractive, rather than on whether it "fits" the world better.[31] An activity like science or philosophy has value only in terms of its success or failure to get it to do what we want it to do. For this reason we are right to judge science according to whether it satisfies our urge to maximize the experimental character of

---

[29] "Solidarity or Objectivity?," p. 33.
[30] See "Non-Reductive Physicalism" in *Objectivism, Relativism and Truth*, pp. 124–5.
[31] *Contingency Irony and Solidarity*, p. 6.

our way of life. Scientists have no more secure standards of inquiry other than the hope of redescribing the world in which their endeavours will have to prove their utility.[32] Consequently, there is no criterion for its utility other than to keep the experimental process open.

EXPERIMENTALISM AND COMMUNITY
IN RORTY'S LIBERALISM

Much of what Rorty wants from a pragmatic re-interpretation of intellectual culture is borrowed from Dewey. He must therefore try to overcome some of the problems and the inconsistencies that plague Dewey's own work. Dewey often writes as if science were simply an investigation of causes which could serve as an unproblematic instrument for improving the consciousness and justice of the self-regulation of human ideals. Yet he also claims that social interests are represented in science not by the aim of objectivity (which results from correct procedure) but by the openness and creativity of the experimental process itself.[33] According to this conception there is no difference between science and the attempt to make society's self-understanding more open to experiment and critical re-interpretation. This transformation of self-understanding cannot occur by virtue of an instrumentalization of science itself but only by virtue of an effectively expressed public need which has indicated to inquirers which consequences are to be considered worthy of attention.

However, it has been argued that Dewey should have realized that there is no *naturally* democratic role for science, unless, from the start, science is conceived as the social and political liberation of public self-understanding. From this point of view science cannot be said to serve democracy simply by making public intelligence and communication more effective; rather the criterion of effective communication would have to be identified in the first place with the political struggle to make communication function critically. Considerations like these led Habermas, in his earlier work on the theory of knowledge, to try to

---

[32] This point is driven home most forcefully by Rorty's conception of "edifying discourse" in *Philosophy and the Mirror of Nature*.

[33] Dewey, *The Public and its Problems*, p. 201ff.

isolate an interest in emancipation, separate from the interest in technical control and mutual understanding. Dewey, however, suggests that the reason we want scientists to pose questions like, 'Why and how do some needs and interests get more public recognition than others?' is because the results of such inquiry will furnish a knowledge of social laws that will help create better instruments for achieving our ends.[34] However, if a theory of society is to have an emancipatory interest it is not because it can serve as a tool for social engineering, but because it must be oriented toward defending or critically examining the grounds of a society's normative commitments or power arrangements. This was essentially Habermas' point when he expressed reservations not only about Weber's separation of science and politics but also about some aspects of Dewey's overconfident view of the democratic meaning of the "scientization of politics."[35]

More recently this problem has been noticed by Marion Smiley who has shown that Dewey moves too easily between two models of science.[36] On the one hand science is a kind of technical organ of social self-control and provides a way for human beings to monitor increasingly complex experiences. On the other hand it is a model for a publicly intelligent community which requires democratically structured input in order to distinguish, in an appropriate way, desirable from undesirable consequences. According to Smiley, Dewey simply identified science and democracy as equivalent ways to determine which questions to pose, which causes and consequences to investigate and regulate. He obviously did so in order to do away with the troubling distinction between the objective discovery of consequences and value-criticism itself. From Weber's perspective, intellectual integrity would be compromised if science were to become an instrument of democratic social engineering. He believed science could serve moral forces only by independently promoting the aim of clarifying the implications of controversial value-choices. For this reason he separated science from democratic politics. The attempt to borrow the idea of liberal

---

[34] Ibid., p. 197.

[35] Habermas, *Toward a Rational Society*, p. 66.

[36] See Marion Smiley, "Pragmatic Inquiry and Social Conflict: A Critical Reconstruction of Dewey's Model of Democracy."

democracy from the ideal scientific community would simply ignore the fateful competition between the 'gods' of science and politics characteristic of our disenchanted world. If one were to allow public opinion to function freely within science then it could simply become the handmaiden of powerful political interests in the name of becoming a democratizing force. There would be nothing to allow us to distinguish the 'scientific' adequacy of our present consciousness of consequences from whatever value choices have been or can be made to seem attractive to us. Public opinion seemed to him to be in conflict with the scientific responsibility to clarify independently the implications of those value choices.

It is only in those moments when Dewey defines democracy *as* a struggle over competing value premises that he is able to develop consistently the experimental side of liberal democracy that he expected science to establish in actual social and political affairs. Science is the ideal method of democracy because it compels critical revisions of communally binding value choices and distinctions among desirable and undesirable consequences. However, Dewey often remarks that the point of democracy is that there is no ideal political method, only experimental methods for arriving at new interpretations, or "symbols," that could guide social problem-solving. This is the point that Rorty wants to retain from Dewey's social theory—the priority of democracy *over* science and philosophy. But he must try to dissociate himself from Dewey's idea that science is the ideal way of considering symbols and interpretive achievements as actual or potential objects of struggle and controversy. Science has no privileged way of deciding whether desirable or undesirable consequences have been defined well or poorly since this depends upon political judgements that are the result of public discussion. Likewise, when he sought to articulate a political ideal Dewey relied upon the curiously trans-political observation that "democracy...is the idea of community life itself."[37] Indeed Dewey often simply begged the most important questions altogether, praising democracy as the most effective way of openly clarifying how we should share our fate with others, while in the same breath saying that

---

[37] *The Public and its Problems*, p. 149.

true community exists only among those who already share a conception of the good life.[38]

The paradoxes threatening the pragmatist commitment to experimental democracy are seemingly built into its theory of truth. As we have seen, the pragmatist defines truth by the usefulness of the beliefs that result from the experimental process. But when pragmatists speak of the 'usefulness' of political freedom to *our* way of life they are suggesting that the way we decide how issues become politically relevant in the first place is already built into our socialization. Pragmatists like Rorty argue that when it comes to determining where the public interest lies, liberalism requires us to respond in a politically neutral way to issues that belong in the private realm, such as those that touch upon our projects of self-realization and self-creation. Of course, these issues are not totally independent from political questions such as 'Whose self-realization should matter to us?' or 'Why are you willing to promote these values over those?' or "Is this an issue about which people can disagree peacefully?" In Rorty's terms we leave these questions to be answered by our free and open encounters, not so much because we "should" but because we have the institutions that allow us to do so successfully.

But Rorty does not himself make the separation between public and private issues so easy for himself. At the moment when we doubt the adequacy of the terms or the 'final vocabulary' in which we express these questions, we must fall back on our decision to affirm or reject our contingent selves. On such occasions politics loses its neutral character. Indeed, Rorty claims that politics should be neutral toward competing conceptions of the good, but that ultimately politics can only be defined in a communitarian way, as a non-neutral decision about whether we should continue to affirm those values that have informed

---

[38] As Dewey writes: "Wherever there is conjoint activity whose consequences are appreciated as good by all singular persons who take part in it, and where the realization of the good is such as to effect an energetic desire and effort to sustain it in being just because it is a good shared by all, there is in so far a community. The clear consciousness of a communal life, in all its implications, constitutes the idea of a democracy." *The Public and its Problems*, p. 149.

our socialization. His conception of politics is clearly derived from his definition of a "final vocabulary":

> It is 'final' in the sense that if doubt is cast on the worth of these words, their user has no noncircular argumentative recourse. Those words are as far as he can go with language; beyond them there is only helpless passivity or a resort to force. A small part of a final vocabulary is made up of thin, flexible, and ubiquitous terms such as "true", "good," "right," and "beautiful." The larger part contains thicker, more rigid, and more parochial terms, for example, "Christ," "England," "professional standards," "decency," "kindness," "the Revolution," "the Church," "progressive," "rigorous," "creative." The more parochial terms do most of the work.[39]

This explains why pragmatists like Dewey and Rorty fall back on a communitarian conception of politics (including democratic politics in Dewey's case). They believe that the purpose of liberal democratic politics is to expand our recognition of the kinds of problems, needs and desires that can be taken into account in our public actions and decisions. On the other hand, politics ultimately depends upon our ability to express what we affirm and what we reject. Rorty's liberal community therefore draws the line between morality and prudence based on what is useful to its way of life even though its adherence to liberalism seems to require it to keep open the question of whether a change in what we consider to be useful to the community's way of life would itself be desirable. The communitarian conception of politics would therefore come into conflict with the ideal goals of moral and political experimentation favoured by liberalism.[40]

For Rorty this apparent problem of self-referential paradox can be evaded.[41] The paradox disappears when we realize that the point of liberal democracy and of the pragmatist theory of truth is always to keep open the question of what kind of identity we want to have. Our acceptance of public indeterminacy and "lightmindedness" in matters of

---

[39] *Contingency, Irony and Solidarity*, p. 73.
[40] On this problem see Walzer, "The Communitarian Critique of Liberalism," pp. 6–23.
[41] Rorty, "On Ethnocentrism: A Reply to Clifford Geertz" in *Objectivity, Relativism and Truth*, p. 207.

truth has become our liberal democratic ideal only because we have learned to use it to "help along the disenchantment of the world."[42]   He therefore believes that it is the disenchantment of the world brought about by modern institutions of secular freedom which has given us a more "attractive" view of truth, a view that allows us to say that we are the kind of people who are willing to call truth whatever results from free and open encounters.   We can give no better explanation for this perspective than that one set of challenges have simply replaced those challenges previously associated with the questions of philosophers.

It can be said that Rorty's is a moral perspectivism of the type Alexander Nehamas has found in Nietzsche.   According to Nehamas, the moral perspectivist "give[s] up the very idea of trying to determine in general terms the value of life and the world...and turn[s] to oneself in order to make one's life valuable without claiming that one's particular method for accomplishing this end should, or even could, be followed by others."[43]   The implication of this view is that there is separation, but no necessary conflict, between the search for private perfection and the dictates of liberal public morality recommending tolerance and understanding of other perspectives.   The members of Rorty's ideal liberal society would be committed to operate publically within the boundaries of a common "final vocabulary," but would find the ideal of truth an unhelpful "nuisance" to shape the course of our "free and open encounters" and publicly accountable actions.   For ours is a culture in which "freedom is the recognition of contingency."   We liberals have come to the point of redescribing our intellectual and moral progress not as the discovery of the truth but as planting the right metaphors in the right place at the right time.

Rorty argues that nominalism does not have to lead to despair about the absence of any value perspective to justify science or the intellectual life.   The most serious task of intellectual life is not the search for truth but the process of inventing more attractive stories about who we are and what we want to become.   According to Rorty, Freud captured the liberating side of the ironist's wisdom with his notion that the goal of

---

[42] "The Priority of Democracy to Philosophy" in *Objectivity, Relativism and Truth*, p. 193.
[43] Nehamas, *Nietzsche: Life as Literature*, pp. 136–35.

seeking the 'truth' amounts to putting ourselves in a position to "re-describe" our options as persons.[44] The goal of the process is to "become those who we are." For a pragmatist, the imperative to "become those who we are" is as central as it is to Nietzsche. Dewey and Rorty, no less than Nietzsche, mean to affront the 'philosophers' with the claim that, if there is 'truth,' it is really the result of a convenient experimental process. The value of the institutions or means involved lies in the fact that they do not presuppose the prior existence of a program by which the growth and creativity of human selves and communities can be promoted.

In this sense, then, the 'truth' has no higher standing than our ability to create ourselves out of the contingencies that we are. It was probably in reference to this idea that Theodore Adorno suggested that Deweyan pragmatism indeed marks a "wholly humane" model of philosophy. But he also accompanied this remark with the claim that pragmatism yields to the temptation of "renouncing philosophy, from the outset, in favour of the test it has to stand."[45]   Rorty would consider himself immune from this criticism, for he believes that he has pushed all the interesting questions to the meta-philosophical level. Rorty freely admits that in the new historicist culture the term "rational" would have no other meaning than "internal coherence." He proposes that philosophy should break free altogether from what Nietzsche called the "spirit of seriousness" since the human mind has nothing more fundamental to discover about itself than the implications of the rhetorical strategies it has created.

But Rorty's critics have charged that his end-of-philosophy theory has implications that contradict his own liberalism; for they surmise that his liberalism masks a perspective that Adorno despised in Heidegger's

---

[44] Rorty, "Freud and Moral Reflection" pp. 143–163.

[45] Theodore Adorno, *Negative Dialectics*, p. 14; As for Rorty's characterization of this side of Dewey's thought he writes: "Dewey was accused of blowing up the optimism and flexibility of a parochial and jejune way of life (the American) into a philosophical system. So he did, but his reply was that *any* philosophical system is going to be an attempt to express the ideals of *some* community's way of life. He was quite ready to admit that the virtue of his philosophy was, indeed, nothing more than the virtue of the way of life which it commended." (Rorty, "Science as Solidarity," p. 43.); Cf. Dewey, *Philosophy and Civilization*, pp. 13–35.

"ontologization of history"—namely, that "nothing remains but the naked affirmation of what is anyway—the affirmation of power."[46] Recent critical theorists like Thomas McCarthy and Richard Bernstein ask directly of Rorty whether pragmatists themselves would really be attracted to a version of their philosophy that praises liberal openness but practices parochialism. McCarthy writes in his exchange with Rorty:

> Citing Peirce, Rorty urges us to think of our beliefs as rules of action *rather than* as candidates for unconditional validity. But Peirce proposed no either/or. What rule of action, he might have asked, is implicated in the view that beliefs are not candidates for unconditional validity? Rorty provides us with a clue: we are to "give up on 'transcultural validity'" and ask "not whether a claim can be 'rationally defended' but whether it can be made to cohere with a sufficient number of *our* beliefs and desires". Thus one of the rules in question seems to be: don't engage in radical criticism of *our* culture and society.[47]

McCarthy is asking what happens to the *liberal* commitment to critical reflection when the need for "practical confidence"[48] in our contingently produced identity becomes a more important moral-political criterion than our capacity for reason (that is, the capacity to make free responses to criticizable validity claims). In my concluding chapter it will be important to consider, among other things, whether the emphasis on the mere cultural success of liberal democracy invites a certain cynicism toward the public realization of its moral aims.

---

[46] *Negative Dialectics*, pp. 130-31.
[47] Thomas McCarthy, "Ironist Theory as a Vocation: A Response to Rorty's Reply," p. 648.
[48] I borrow this term from Bernard Williams, *Ethics and The Limits of Philosophy*, p. 171, where he puts it to very subtle use in developing his ideas about the reasons for the tension between reflection and socialization in ethics.

Chapter Seven

ON THE MORAL CONTINGENCY OF LIBERAL DEMOCRATIC POLITICS

Max Weber proposed that a certain kind of victory had been achieved by liberalism in the process of rationalization that has brought about the disenchantment of the world. At the same time he described this as a hollow victory, since liberalism has survived in a world in which its moral claims have become less salient than its (possible) functional advantages. We have seen that for Weber a culturally successful liberal democracy could at most provide a context for a struggle between bureaucrats and leaders. Strauss (and Bloom more recently) suggests that Weber and Nietzsche were the unwitting precursors of a shameless politicization of liberal cultural institutions that has made intellectual integrity compatible with permissiveness. With Rorty, however, the distance from Nietzsche and Weber has increased with happier results; liberal democrats are now returning as the vanguard of the new intellectual situation.[1] Indeed he claims that there has been no better opportunity for a morally self-confident commitment to pluralism and political freedom than the historicist realization that there is no ahistorical or unconditioned way of deciding among competing truths, values or beliefs. But he also claims that our commitment to liberal ideals is perfectly compatible with the idea that the moral life of our community is bounded by the contingent "final vocabulary" to which we have adapted.

---

[1] See his review of Bloom's *The Closing of the American Mind* entitled "Straussianism, Democracy and Allan Bloom,"

AN ENVIRONMENT FOR IRONISTS

As we have seen, one way in which Rorty tries to neutralize the troubling implications of his ethnocentrism is to say that our sense of who 'we' are—that is, 20th century members of wealthy liberal democratic societies—includes the recognition that our final vocabulary is only as good as its capacity to become a context for public tolerance and private self-creation. Nietzsche has much to offer 'our kind' at least if we understand him to be saying that we need not abandon attempts at self-knowledge or truth altogether, but should rather identify them with attempts at self-creation.[2]   He therefore helped modern intellectuals abandon "the idea of finding a single context for all human lives." What is promising about Nietzsche is that he could still intimate a teaching about what kind of human powers matter most.[3]   What is objectionable about Nietzsche, however, was his last-ditch attempt to transcend historicism altogether, with his alleged discovery of a type of human being whose life represents the completion of human powers. Rorty also takes exception to a thinker like Foucault who, although he shares Rorty's idea that all truths are the product and instrument of specific contexts, was led to assume that the problems of his society could *only* be authentically addressed ironically, and that the mark of a genuine intellectual was to refuse to be defined by a political and ethical tradition.[4]

In short, Rorty warns against following Nietzschean scepticism toward human solidarity and socialization. As we have seen, in Rorty's ideal liberal society the ironic sensibilities that inform the aspiration toward idiosyncratic self-creation in the modern world would not be given the last word in assessing the worth of moral and political beliefs themselves. He envisages a society which is a "safe haven" for ironists rather than an invitation for them to create forms for everyone else. But what has aroused the objections of his critics is that he does not rely on a moral defense of his separation of private irony and the beliefs and practices for which one is publicly accountable. Instead he simply

---

[2] *Contingency, Irony and Solidarity*, pp. 28ff.
[3] Ibid., p. 27.
[4] "Moral Identity and Private Autonomy," in *Essays on Heidegger and Others*, p. 195.

characterizes irony as an implausible model of society: "I cannot imagine a culture which socialized its young in such a way as to make them continually dubious about their own process of socialization."[5]

But for Rorty the solution is not to abandon the teachings of theorists like Nietzsche and Weber, but only to reconsider their implications. Like Strauss he argues that the social glue that binds us to our moral community can only have pseudo-natural and pseudo-rational foundations. But unlike Strauss and Nietzsche he claims that our inability to find any non-contingent standards against which our communal attachments can be evaluated need not make us equally suspect of all moral and political values.

Rorty of course is well aware that the philosophical sceptic, or the "ironist" in his terms, need not automatically be a liberal. He or she might want to find a more dangerous public application for his or her model of "self-overcoming and self-invention." In doing so the ironist transgresses the "banal moral vocabulary" of liberalism, a vocabulary which is valuable only because it is suited to the uniquely public purpose of arranging and exploring "compromises among persons."[6] Rorty is therefore preoccupied with the problem of describing our historicist age so that private irony will readily identify itself as the complement of public liberalism. To do this, however, he must find a way to make a virtue out of his sharp distinction between the two realms. He must dispel the idea that the public morality of liberalism provides a free ride for those who have the most effective strategies of (rhetorical) power. He therefore tries to show why liberal solidarity would itself be historicist and nominalistic, harmlessly open to the provocation of ironists rather than an instrument to be cynically manipulated by them. A fundamental aspect of our cultural self-understanding would be based on an acknowledgement that, in the words of Bernard Williams, "any determinate ethical outlook is going to represent some kind of specialization of human possibilities."[7] The ironist would therefore be one of the "character types" encouraged by liberal democracy. He or she has a more specialized view of the

---

[5] *Contingency, Irony and Solidarity*, p. 87.

[6] "Moral Identity and Private Autonomy," p. 196.

[7] Williams, *Ethics and the Limits of Philosophy*, p. 153.

culture, one which is spent combating complacency, comparatively examining contingent "final vocabularies" (as an ethnologist, for example) or subjecting one's own final vocabulary to playful self-doubt through literature. But this ironist would not undermine the environment sustained by liberal democratic morality, since she gains much from the formation of a general public which is increasingly aware of historical contingency. Indeed such awareness would be a sign of the political and moral maturity with which liberal citizens commit themselves to their arrangements (such as an "overlapping consensus") rather than a reason for self-doubt.[8]

If one is a nominalist/historicist, and one believes that one's attachment to the moral goals of one's society needs no justification, one does not have to draw the conclusion that morality is meaningless. According to Rorty this is because members of our society have already acquired the "non-metaphysical commonsense"[9] to know that the point of morality is to mark off "the sort of people one wants to be from the sort of person one does not want to be."[10]   The case of the ironist is different but convergent.   The ironist *would* want to be a liberal for public purposes because he or she knows that the history of moral and intellectual progress can be most forcefully told to fellow members of the society so as to inspire their curiosity, that is, to portray it as the story of idiosyncratic ways of speaking and acting which have prevailed because of a lucky combination of historical circumstances.[11]   Such stories would provoke people to enrich their mode of solidarity by asking more pointed questions about themselves. Successful provocation does not imply the aim of undermining solidarity altogether.

Likewise the kind of liberal democracy Dewey identified as a politics informed by experimental and fallibilistic thought would be a suitable environment for ironists. In particular it would allow them room to specialize in self-invention (as poets and revolutionaries) and in disclosing the pseudo-natural quality of their communal attachments (as novelists, journalists and psychoanalysts). At the same time, the ironist

---

[8] *Contingency, Irony and Solidarity*, p. 87.
[9] Ibid.
[10] Ibid., p. 47.
[11] Ibid., p. 37.

would share with the rest of his or her society a taste for a public life which would resist the search for an objective ordering of values, while providing a viable identity: "[T]he ironist, the person who has doubts about his own final vocabulary, his own moral identity, and perhaps his own sanity—desperately needs to *talk* to other people, needs this with the same urgency as people need to make love."[12]   This exemplifies Rorty's belief that the point of moral openness is not to tie either private or political freedom to the purification of communicative intentions. Most importantly, this radical Socratic questioning would not have a Platonic resolution, it cannot be thought of as leading to the discovery of a moral purpose—or a reinterpretation of nature or history—more fitting for human life in general.   Rather it simply makes available a more interesting setting for developing tools for enriching the vocabulary which "we" have been lucky enough to have at our disposal by virtue of our socialization and inherited culture.   Part of what makes us lucky is that our moral tool-kit is differentiated enough to allow us to place our "erotic relationships" side by side with our social responsibilities.

MORAL ISSUES AND
STRONG CONTINGENCY

In the previous section I have tried to portray Rorty's combination of irony and liberalism in a way that aims at smoothing over some of the alleged inconsistencies noted by his critics.   However, questions linger about whether his version of a liberal consensus is workable *and* desirable, even if we grant that he has evaded philosophical objections. Can ironists and those mundane historicists who have been more routinely socialized coexist, especially since each type will evidently have to feel "lucky" for different reasons?   If there is a strong argument against Rorty it is that he implies that we can be liberal democrats or Nietzschean supermen for no other reasons than that it suits the purposes we happen to have.   Again, Rorty responds to this argument by saying that, for the kind of society he has in mind, relativization of criteria would simply be a non-issue, rather than the path toward a cynical way

---

[12] Ibid., p. 186.

of life. But in the face of such claims one is led to suspect that Rorty's account of what makes our culture successful is circular. By becoming historicist we will want to get along without asking philosophers to come up with "an intrinsic set of powers to be developed or left undeveloped."[13] But if 'we' have a successful culture perhaps it is simply because 'we' are not embarrassed to live in a society that actively makes us conscious of contingency (and tries to re-program us accordingly).

Critics of Rorty can easily contend that while we recognize that there are other ways of ordering one's own system of values, Rorty's ideal society of liberals is like any other culture—although it preaches tolerance of other ways of life, it is unable to go beyond its own way of adapting to contingencies. But as Strauss would no doubt argue, we need a more prudent system of moral restraint which could compose a reliable dividing line between the art of questioning convention and consensus on the one hand, and the practice of social responsibility on the other. The alternative is to remain content simply with intellectual integrity. If this standard is the only legitimate one for criticism it must exclude from the start the possibility of finding a privileged standpoint. Intellectual integrity means that we have to be dogmatic, since we cannot avoid making intellectual sacrifices. Indeed, Richard Bernstein, who is positioned on the philosophical "left," has criticized Rorty's "fideism" just as strongly as any Straussian would. Rorty's response is that we have no choice but to compare standpoints in terms of the contingent difference between the questions one finds interesting and those one does not.[14] From the standpoint of a critical social theory that would hold liberalism to its own standards, this difference cannot be contingent.

Rorty insists that the decline of the philosophical ethos does not entail the decline of an ethical commitment to the liberal way of life. In

---

[13] Ibid., p. 35.

[14] For Strauss there are fundamental problems, most notably that of the alternative between revelation and reason. But there is no way of *grounding* the project of philosophy since any attempt to ground it merely presupposes it. Hence philosophy is an infinite conversation. On these and similar points see Stanley Rosen, "Leo Strauss and the Quarrel between the Ancients and the Moderns," *Leo Strauss' Thought: Toward a Critical Engagement*, ed. A. Udoff, pp. 155–168.

fact, Rorty claims that political and ethical reflection can and need have no other basis than exploring, refining and re-describing the "practical advantages" of the ethnocentrically self-defining order one inhabits. When some intellectuals in a previously 'metaphysical culture' are attracted to the conception of "historical contingency" others will worry about the detachment of politics and morality from free disputes about rationally criticizable validity claims. They will believe that a dangerous relativization of all moral and political reflection follows from the idea that every cultural self-understanding is ultimately supported by nothing other than a self-assertive program to favor the development of certain kinds of persons and institutions and to exclude others. According to Rorty this response is the result of a bad image of moral problems, one which views all moral and political ties as either rationally reconstructible or as the mask of power relations. In his view, only if one believes that historicism implies such an either/or will one also believe that the society open to its own contingency will be consumed by relativism to the point of having no moral or political resources left to prevent the cynical breakdown of the distinction between moral appeals and prudential appeals.

On this issue Rorty argues that we should not place ourselves in the Platonic tradition of trying to answer Thrasymachus' challenge.[15] By this he means that one must acknowledge that each society must put its own responsibility to itself first when drawing the line between morality and prudence. In this conception morality is simply the relation we have to those kinds of people with whom we can hope to have the kind of communicative encounters that even liberal ironists would for their own reasons want to promote in public life, encounters in which the needs and interests of each person are taken in his or her own terms. At several points Rorty suggests that the ideal liberal is one who thinks of herself as an imaginative participant in a potentially infinite number

---

[15] See for example Rorty, "Moral Identity and Private Autonomy: The Case of Foucault," p. 197; See also "Straussianism, Democracy and Allan Bloom," p. 33 where Rorty remarks that "For Deweyans, the theoretical questions 'Did Socrates answer Thrasymachus?' and 'Can we answer Hitler?' get replaced by practical questions like 'How can we arrange things so that people like Thrasymachus and Hitler will not come to power?'"

of conversations. Yet this self-concept would be combined with the realization that everything comes down to whether one can stand up for one's convictions with "sincerity" or "unflinching courage." He or she would be satisfied that "solidarity with all possible vocabularies is impossible," and that "a conviction that could be justified to anyone would be of little interest."[16]   Our interest in morality is then bounded by prudence—it is a matter of justifying oneself to the *relevant* kinds of people. As for our relations to those whose terms, and conversational contributions we cannot take seriously after sincere attempts, they are not moral but prudential.

In this respect it may seem that Rorty's position comes close to that of Carl Schmitt who viewed all moral controversy under the possibility of politics, or decisive friend/enemy relations. For Schmitt there is no such thing as liberal, politically neutral prudence. This would only appear to be possible in the economistic forms of liberalism after Hobbes which set out to neutralize politics.[17] According to Schmitt this kind of liberalism succeeds only in obscuring the highest kind of prudence, that is, the non-neutral public resolve we adopt in those relations which concern our existential interest in friend/enemy groupings. Rorty however does not assert the primacy of self-assertion in politics as does Schmitt. The relevant ethics of community in his liberal society would delimit politics by specializing morality for public purposes since it involves getting along as well as possible with those who pursue incompatible ends or private projects. This is radically opposed to Schmitt's concept of the 'political' as the impossibility of normalizing substantive conflict. Although the lives of people in Rorty's liberal society are necessarily divided between morality and prudence, they would always try to put openness in political controversy ahead of their belief in the necessity of political conflict. Hence, contrary to Schmitt, Rorty argues that all moral questions need not be subsumed under naturally occurring friend/enemy relations. We will not want to ask whether our society or any other is itself a moral society, one whose arrangements express or fail to express some

---

[16] *Contingency, Irony and Solidarity*, pp. 47, 88.
[17] Carl Schmitt, *The Concept of the Political*, p. 68.

fundamental moral truth.[18] This demand is cast aside in favor of trying to shape our political life as much as possible by coming to understand everyone's interests and problems in their own terms. Rorty is fond of reminding us that the world's best "connoisseurs of diversity" come from the "lucky" liberal democratic societies. The key contention here seems to be that the form of cultural self-assertion liberalism adopts has made its adherents the most effective political opponents of intolerance and crude political self-assertion.[19] It is by trial and error, rather than by recognizing the necessity of "resolute decision," that we draw the line between morality and prudence.

It is worth recounting the kind of responses explicitly and implicitly made by Rorty's critics, especially those on the philosophical left, like Habermas, Bernstein and McCarthy. They argue that Rorty's or Weber's view of what liberalism can be must exclude an acknowledgement that the integrity of the life-world itself requires recognition of the normative content of procedures designed to examine beliefs rationally through communicating about criticizable validity claims. While Rorty insists that it makes no sense for historicism to slide into a rejection of liberal democracy neither does he define our appreciation for a liberal democratic community in terms of a reason we might have to affirm the moral purpose of its institutions. Free and open communication is, like markets and procedural impartiality, merely one of the behavioural options we have selected for regulating a way of life "we" happen to find useful. There is nothing to prevent us from finding another final vocabulary more "attractive," one which would cause us to define our political life as either pure struggle, or as the legitimation of social arrangements based on an inflexible, communication-resistant decision to place a dividing line between us and them, or between the kind of values we want to promote and the kind of values we want to fight against.

As for his reply, Rorty disarmingly insists that his view of truth in public affairs is akin to that of Habermas. He praises Habermas and Dewey for championing the view that truth is the name we give to

---

[18] See "Moral Identity and Private Autonomy."

[19] "On Ethnocentrism: A Reply to Clifford Geertz," in *Objectivity, Relativism and Truth*, pp 203–10.

whatever results when a society allows for open and free encounters. But he suggests that Habermas is unwilling to accept that much of what we value in liberalism is attributable to its unintended consequences; that its value has resulted from the opportunity it affords to particularize life contexts and to participate in the process of replacing old vocabularies by new ones. The weakness of Habermas' point of view is that he fails to see how liberal democracies can gain anything by inviting people to tailor their private identities for this purpose. From Rorty's perspective it should not matter that the desirability of openness and freedom may itself be viewed as contingent.[20]   Liberal democratic discussions and moral practices cannot be founded on the basis of the capacity of the ideal speech community to define our hopes by something we all share simply by virtue of our common humanity. On the contrary, liberals only need possibilities and hopes that can be made stronger by making their contingent standards of invention and creativity more self-conscious.

Of course such *strong* contingency is intolerable to Habermas. Rorty concedes that Habermas is his ally in wanting to do away with the metaphysical assumption that truth pre-exists the process of discovery. However, he believes Habermas is wrong to want to replace metaphysics with an equally dubious idea that there is a certain kind of speech we are constrained to use (or that must have priority) in public life if we want to produce a consensus (or outcome) that will pass the test of freedom and openness. For Rorty the point of openness and freedom is to allow experimentation that deals with the possibility of replacing old vocabularies by new ones. He calls this "quest for the sublime...one of the prettier unforced blue flowers of bourgeois culture."[21]   This process, he argues, is not governed by the rules of public argument aiming at consensus but by the constant re-invention of the rules of successful rhetoric. McCarthy responds to this point by arguing that only within the sphere of argumentative speech can the test

---

[20] For criticisms of Rorty on this point see Richard Bernstein, "Rorty's Liberal Utopia"; Cf. Habermas, "Questions and Counterquestions," in *Habermas and Modernity*, ed. R. Bernstein, pp. 194–8.

[21] "Habermas and Lyotard on Postmodernity" in *Essays on Heidegger and Others*, p. 176.

of freedom and openness be considered in a meaningful way. According to him, we cannot take seriously the interests and needs of others in communication without believing that such communication must function, at least in ideal cases, as a reciprocal process of taking positions on freely raised "criticizable validity claims." But for Rorty it would be paradoxical to propose that the test of openness and freedom ought to be used to limit from the start the chance of developing a more innovative form of *cultural* self-assertion, especially when the community in question is defined by the *political* desirability of openness and freedom.

THE POLITICS OF MORAL IDENTITY

Many of the issues in the debate I have been tracing are part of a larger set of concerns recently designated by the term "the politics of identity." For Emile Durkheim and Rousseau, two of the greatest theorists of solidarity, each society's moral truth must correspond to real social forces that condition its identity. For Durkheim this implied that morality is a functional requirement of social order. He claimed that modern society needs new moral truths in order to become adapted to its emergent "final vocabulary" in which our moral-political horizons would be expressed in terms of participation in specialized functional areas.[22] Unlike Durkheim, Rorty does not believe that we can speak of the meaning of our beliefs, values, desires or goals in terms of moral truth. And yet he asserts that the moral sentiment "cruelty is the worst thing we do," as well as our desire not to humiliate others, amount to something like essential functional requirements of liberal democratic solidarity and identity. Of course, even cruelty can be made attractive by re-description. It does not have an "essence," which, for Rorty, is simply one of the reasons the liberal public conversation needs to have its rhetoric enriched in addition to having its processes of argumentation made more open and free.[23]

But it is nevertheless clear that Rorty insists that the aversion to

---

[22] For a useful account of Durkheim's relationship to pragmatism see Edward Tiryakian, *Sociologism and Existentialism*, p. 158ff.

[23] This issue is discussed in depth by Richard Bernstein in his "Rorty's Liberal Utopia," p. 51.

cruelty and humiliation is something like a moral truth for the liberal democratic way of life. Of course there are no moral universals, since, as Rorty argues, our defense of liberalism against a figure like O'Brien in Orwell's *1984* can only be achieved by pitting our rhetoric against his. O'Brien knew that the trick of socialization that makes any final vocabulary 'final' can become more powerful than worries about the true nature or inner meaning of the moral aims expressed by the 'thin', ambiguous terms in that final vocabulary.[24] People like O'Brien can deploy the trick of socialization without even bothering to enter the sphere of morality. They can, in other words, replace morality with rhetoric.[25]

Rorty wants to avoid the negative outcome of disenchantment which O'Brien or 'the Party' represents. He wants to avoid the nightmare situation in which all terms can become relative to whatever is convenient for successful socialization. This is the scenario in which moral dialogue is over before it has begun—the scenario which McCarthy had accused Rorty of promoting. At times he does suggest that the elaboration of moral truths is of independent significance for the moral identity of liberals. For a liberal is someone who cannot engage in debate about social responsibilities without always worrying about enlarging her sensitivity to cruelty, something that, since it refers to a common feature of everyone—the capacity to feel pain and to be used—cannot be considered relative to the terms that describe it or that we use to justify our actions. Bernstein, therefore, has questioned the value of the commitment to avoid cruelty when this area of social problems is so conceived that there can be no rational arguments to produce agreement about what the relevant examples of cruelty and humiliation are.[26] In posing social problems Rorty says we will have to rely upon our non-neutral vocabularies which "do all the work," which designate our hopes and fears, friends and enemies, or heroes and villains. We can only have reference to a communitarian 'we' when discussing the kinds of cruelty and humiliation that are to be avoided.[27]

---

[24] *Contingency, Irony and Solidarity*, p. 175–77.
[25] Ibid., p. 214.
[26] Bernstein "Rorty's Liberal Utopia," p. 63.
[27] *Contingency, Irony and Solidarity*, p. 191–92.

But at this point in the argument the requirement of public neutrality is reintroduced: all 'we' can say about the existence of others who are suffering pain and humiliation is to notice how, with reference to pain and humiliation, they are deprived of having the same hopes we have and to view them as 'candidates' for sharing those hopes. Ours is a culture that keeps separate the vocabularies that deal with our private self-realization and the vocabulary that deals with our public accountability to others. In the former we speak in terms of self-creation, and in the latter we speak in terms of how to build a more inclusive 'we', that is, how to build a world where our morality/prudence distinction will simply be a neutral modus vivendi rather than a trade-off between 'our' goals and 'theirs.'

The goal of public life in Rorty's liberalism is to achieve convenience, largely because liberals are defined as the kind of people who want their excitement, and their self-development, to go on in private. The moral vocabulary and identity that this 'we' would use in public to debate and decide upon its social responsibilities would be "banal" precisely because the common purpose it would be designed to serve is the non-controversial one of avoiding cruelty and humiliation. This does not amount to a rule against criticizing one's own culture, as McCarthy claims, so much as a thinning out of the space of public action and judgement so that only one issue remains—that of our common worry about cruelty—for serious consideration.

Bernstein, has provided an account of what Rorty's liberal democratic public realm would look like.

> [P]olitics, especially liberal politics, must confront the question of what should be done to deal with serious conflicts about cruelty and humiliation. Rorty never thematizes this question. Rorty's politics seems to be one in which there is no public space—the space in which human beings come together to *debate* and *argue* with each other. This is what Dewey (one of Rorty's heroes) called the "eclipse of the public." For public debate presupposes what Rorty seems to want to eliminate— that we can be locked in *argument* with each other.[28]

Bernstein's alternative is a mode of solidarity and justice which could

---

[28] Bernstein, "Rorty's Liberal Utopia," pp. 63–4.

have an independent source in the power of rational discussion, which would encourage people to investigate *why* cruelty and humiliation exists and therefore encourage people to challenge one another to do more than find new terms needed to compare our lives with the lives of people who have been denied 'our' hopes. But Rorty has shown that the value of morality in Bernstein's or Habermas' ideal communication community would require that the public will that is formed in discussion must not be prejudged by the terms of the contingent vocabulary used in it. Rorty suggests, on the contrary, that liberal democracy is the product of a certain kind of successful "prejudgement." One would therefore strip liberal politics of its need to become sensitive to "moral luck,"[29] that is, the need to see our moral goals as the result—not the yardstick—of a discrimination among alternative ways of life (both within liberalism itself and between liberalism and other cultures). He therefore insists that liberalism can only be applied to itself in a pragmatic way, that is, as a particular way of taking responsibility for creating conditions which favour one way of life over another.

The merit of Rorty's work is that he makes us aware of how the politics of identity might become an important dimension of political ethics. However if the aims of his liberal "hero" would, in public life, be similar to those of Nietzsche's banal "last men" it is hard to see how liberalism could have the cultural advantages he claims it does.[30] Indeed, the fact that Rorty's replies to his critics proceed by debunking philosophy through philosophical debate itself reveals some of the limits of his approach. He seems to be insensitive to the fact that whether one is a bland utilitarian nominalist or an ironist intellectual depends to a great extent upon problematic structural features of the prevailing socio-economic arrangements (and systems of power) in our society. More 'traditional' critics of liberalism, including those who would like to see it live up to its promise, have been making this point for a long time, and they probably will not be interested in Rorty's strategy for enriching

---

[29] This term comes from Bernard Williams, *Moral Luck* and *Ethics and the Limits of Philosophy*.

[30] This point is made in an unforgiving critique of Rorty by Sheldon Wolin, "Democracy in the Discourse of Postmodernism," p. 21.

a moral vocabulary that must be supplemented by public neutrality precisely because it makes some people feel lucky with less room for self-realization and others with more.

This is the kind of problem to which Habermas' work is addressed, even though he often employs misplaced philosophical insights for dealing with the problems of political identity. Habermas insists that the kind of vocabulary that would prevail in Rorty's liberal discussions can be said to be arbitrary rather than contingent. This is because we inhabit a "final vocabulary" that is designed for those who are worried more about humiliating people—failing to understand them in their own terms—than about confronting the basic structural sources of injustice. It programs us to be content with the fact that, although the terms in which people see their own interests and desires are never neutral, we could be given assurance that the public realm is structured so as to render this non-neutrality as harmless as possible. This evokes the negative politics of Locke and Madison who wanted to make our tendency to be judges in our own case harmless. In Rorty's work this virtual emasculation of public life is sustained in a curious complementary relationship to his intention to combat complacency in discourse. It overshadows his valuable suggestion that what should interest us about liberal public dialogue is not its capacity to delineate purely formal rules guaranteeing that the equal dignity of each participant will be recognized, but rather to keep us aware that the standards for evaluating *the success or failure* of that dialogue cannot be determined in advance.

ALTERNATIVES AND CONCLUSIONS

Whatever the merits of his proposals, our discussion of Rorty helps a great deal in considering once again the consequences of Weber's characterization of a liberal political culture. Here it is helpful to recall Weber's distinction between the ethics of conviction and the ethics of responsibility. This model suggested that the modern belief that human beings ought to be distinguished by their capacity for rational autonomy in practical life betrayed a fundamental irony in human affairs—namely that one must account not only for how one chooses but for how one confronts the necessity to choose. For instance, one must either choose a life defined by the consistency with which one commits oneself to ultimate ends, or else concern oneself with the effectiveness with which one realizes them. Political action involves tilting toward the latter while respecting the motivating force of the former in human affairs. For Weber this distinction was accompanied by other observations troubling to liberal democratic theorists. He noted that successful moral-political belief-systems, even when they are founded in the name of justice, must in the end serve to validate or promote forces of selection in a society. This view, and his definition of the state as the monopoly of legitimate violence, led him to say that politics deals with morally dubious means. In politics not everyone is going to have control of (or the ability to change) the terms one uses to justify one's life, one's ultimate values or one's advantage. The latter depends upon luck and natural gifts (as in charisma) or power (the supposedly necessary hierarchy in the modern division of labour). According to Weber's sociology, one cannot take responsibility for the success of liberal democracy without first being prepared to deal with the factors of circumstance and power in politics, administration and the dominant patterns of socialization.

Some writers have recently contested Weber's sociological account of the necessary "expropriation of politics" while claiming that one need not totally dispense with Weber's insights about the moral paradoxes of politics.[31] Portis, for example, has argued that Weber's concept of charismatic leadership does not lead to a necessary expropriation of politics for the simple fact that it recognizes the importance of identity-forming symbols in politics as opposed to specific policy considerations. In highly differentiated societies the public has a low threshold for information dealing with policy, but nevertheless has a capacity to learn more effectively how to deal with political information through its response and input into the symbolic dimension of leadership politics. Portis realizes that the alternative concept of "cultural democracy" cannot be sociologically consistent with ideal conditions for the moral practical rationalization of public participation. All it can do is remind

---

[31] A very insightful attempt to 'save' Weber for democratic politics is to be found in Peter Breiner, "Democratic Autonomy, Political Ethics and Moral Luck," *Political Theory.*"

us that the moral riskiness, or moral openness, of politics is constantly reproduced by the question of who is in a position to control the formation of 'final vocabularies'.

> If "cultural democracy" is to mean anything, it must be established that democratic practices make possible a significant degree of popular control of the content and effective use of politically relevant symbols. The citizens rather than the leaders must be able to determine what is to be considered an "award." If elites have a relatively free hand in defining what is estimable, which means that they would have the ability and inclination to apply meaningful symbols in whatever manner they find convenient, or even to cynically manufacture them as needed, then cultural democracy is a sham.[32]

When he turned his mind away from moral paradoxes, and toward moral openness, Weber himself was inclined to argue that the institutionalization of open competition for political success was just as likely to channel charisma in a democratic direction as an authoritarian one.[33] But here, even if we no longer assume the expropriation of politics, the fortunes of popular control no longer lie solely with moral appeals to the public's capacity for more direct participation or critical judgement.

Today's most perspicacious political sociologists see the problems of liberal democratic politics in a similar way. According to Luhmann, for instance, what is important today is to see how democracy has been developed according to the functional differentiation of politics. Under these conditions modern democracy paradoxically copes with the moral demand to learn how to become sensitive to change or public opinion—specifically, by producing its own kind of information. Effective parliamentary democracy increases the chance that criticism of the political system will no longer be overgeneralized, and therefore no longer become a matter of asking whether officials or rulers can be accused of exploiting insecurity or abusing power. Rather, the public realm itself must create specialized means for producing changes in the system's own sensitivity to its environment.[34] It cannot avoid self-referential criteria for success. Luhmann argues that many new

---

[32] Edward Portis, "Charismatic Leadership and Cultural Democracy," p. 241.
[33] *Economy and Society*, vol. 1, p. 266.
[34] Niklas Luhmann, *Political Theory in the Welfare State*, p. 186.

problems are produced by self-referentiality, such as the media's role in forming the political agenda, and the fact that modern electoral politics often promotes short-term over long-term perspectives. But he tends to share Weber's view that the real hope for democracy is that it will not be looked at as legitimation in terms of values, but as a counterweight to bureaucracy. Indeed Luhmann goes further than Weber by arguing that the virtue of democratic politics is precisely the impossibility of codifying the "instability at the top" in terms of the opposition between rulers and ruled.[35] To deal with their inability to master a 'complex' environment (composed of other autonomous systems) modern political systems have instead had to reproduce themselves in operational terms by recodifying democratic politics—and therefore the conditions of democracy's own cultural success—in terms of a binary opposition between government and opposition. This new coding no longer allows the ethics of responsibility to exempt itself from democracy and to promote what Luhmann calls a "'sovereign' distance from morality." Although he goes beyond Weber in many respects, Luhmann is in fundamental agreement with the basic thrust of Weber's political writings on leadership democracy in recommending "the renunciation of the moralizing of political antagonism" as an advance for democracy.[36]

It can be said that Weber, Rorty and Luhmann have each tried to 'redescribe' the cultural success of liberal democratic morality by its more or less open sensitivity to change and innovation that must, however, be interpreted in morally contingent terms. It is no longer possible to accept the Rousseauian model in which the criterion of moral responsibility in politics lies in the capacity of political participants to submit themselves freely, along with their modes of thought and deliberation, to the process of forming general norms that could be considered valid by all. For Rousseau the criterion of morality was the general will itself, which establishes the normative validity of political enactments purely by our disinterested participation in them. It is easy to see that this formulation leaves open many of the questions having to do with the politics of participation and decision-making, as well as struggles over the distribution of political competence and the

---

[35] Ibid., p. 234.
[36] Ibid., p. 237.

responsibility for defining and solving social problems. But more importantly, the very ideal of a democratic republic entails the moral contingency and openness of the political outcome of disinterested participation. The ideal of democracy based on the principle that the "general will cannot err" would have to find an extra-democratic competence for making judgements and decisions about moral risks, hence Rousseau's appeal to "the legislator." For a democracy can never be ideal, if this means bringing its prudential actions under moral considerations. The authority of the legislator must be appealed to on those matters about which the will of the people cannot be disinterested, namely, the options which will have been excluded or promoted through the enactment of their true will.

Perhaps Hannah Arendt has afforded the best, post-Rousseauian response to worries that theories of the moral contingency of politics will lead to cynicism regarding public life. She argued that action oriented to political freedom must be *primarily* defined by the contingency of its results and subsequent conditions.[37] She also argued that the public *impartiality* necessary for radically democratic politics would be based on nothing other than an exacting *partiality* for free and open discussion. But she thereby proposed that the freedom (and equality) specific to the public realm must be created by the participants themselves (and is therefore not a matter of fictionally identifying with their common humanity), and that it only lasts so long as it both separates and relates them as exemplary partners in self-display. This is not the place for an examination of the details of Arendt's thought. But a sufficient indication of the need for a more challenging definition of political freedom and participation lies in the fact that Arendt—who was against all forms of expropriating politics—nevertheless believed that even the strongest traditions of democracy would still have to prove themselves as effective proving grounds for political talent, judgement and sophistication. These traditions, she suggested, might therefore be best served by a certain rarification of politics, albeit one that is anti-bureaucratic and non-expropriative.[38]

---

[37] Arendt, *The Human Condition*, pp. 190ff.
[38] Arendt, *On Revolution*, pp. 275ff.

We can then say that liberal democracy stands to be improved by the recognition of contingency, not simply for the sociological reason that the means of its political realization are morally dubious, but because, as Peter Breiner has put it, "to deliberate and choose public policies in common [is] not just the realization of autonomy and community but also a necessary education to ambiguity of outcome and constant political struggle against routinized domination."[39]

To make headway here we must realize that Weber's account of the irresistability of bureaucracy in modernity is no longer applicable (if it ever was). Indeed it is interesting that students in contemporary schools of administrative studies are currently being taught a similar lesson about the fate of conventional business and professional practices. The success of the modern business enterprise is now said to depend upon the introduction of more participatory values in work and administration. The advent of new technologies have demanded increased attention to the importance of "human capital," and adaptability to change, at all levels of organization. Due to the replacement of standardized mass production by "flexible systems production" one no longer can justify the technical necessity for a hierarchical division of labour. There is now a strong demand, on purely functional grounds, for more decentralization of responsibilities for decisions and learning as well as calls, by a U.S. president, for "investments in people." In fact the platitudinous moralization of these demands has come from the business community which has often joined the call for reform in the manner of a public relations exercise. They believe that the "re-structuring" which must take place in an era of global competition requires a shift away from the welfare state toward a system which would not divert resources from a more socially flexible, privately controlled investment in change. They apparently fail to see that the social freedoms and equity for which contemporary liberal democracy is designed does not simply aim at controlling the 'output' of socio-economic change (guaranteeing equality of results at the cost of efficiency), it also enriches its human 'input' as the new post-bureaucratic model requires.[40] Pure capitalism, advanced in the name of

---

[39] Breiner, "Democratic Autonomy, Political Ethics and Moral Luck," p. 571.

[40] Daniel Bell fails to recognize this point in his "Liberalism in the Postindustrial

flexibility, involves a decrease in human flexibility, to say nothing of human freedom. As we have seen, a similar criticism can be levelled at Parson's defense of a social system that would make trust, as an alternative to hierarchical power, the basis of authority. In any case, a revised version of Weber's ethic of responsibility would have to take into account not only the illusory nature of the belief in the necessity of expropriating politics, but also the current political *necessity* for increased participation.[41]

It would take us far beyond the scope of the present discussion to show further how a revised ethic of responsibility would call for a transformation, rather than a complacent neglect, of our political culture and contemporary liberal democracy. We must recognize that the preconditions of a more successful political culture will have to be conceived in a way that overturns many of Weber's assumptions, including that of the "soullessness of the masses." At the same time, however, we will do well to follow Weber's scepticism toward the anti-democratic 'pathos of distance' characteristic of Nietzsche and today's political and cultural conservatives.

In light of these considerations we must remember that Max Weber's work was attuned to the likelihood that bureaucracy and irresponsible power politics would promote forces of "selection" that would be undesirable from the standpoint of the type of individuality to which he personally adhered. For him, questions of individuality in politics were ultimately to be separated from questions of rights, self-determination or even allowance for the needs of social identity. This may appear to yield too much ground to the Burke-inspired right-wing critics of liberal democracy who champion a kind of "sociological realism," and thereby challenge the commitment to a society founded upon rational consensus, free discussion or egalitarian participation. However, Weber's legacy is not consistent with the Burkean foundations of neo-conservatism in that he remained unwilling to remedy the discrepancy between the effectiveness of values and the question of their validity.

However Weber's work is to be understood or criticized, we might

---

Society" in Bell, *The Winding Path*, p. 236.

[41] Cf. H.T. Wilson in *Political Management: Redefining the Public Sphere.*

nevertheless appreciate his unwillingness to resolve the discrepancy between ideal and reality. We have seen, for example, that the liberal principle of discursive freedom cannot be applied to itself without paradoxes. The standard by which the success of a liberal public dialogue can be judged would be its openness to the possibility that any such standards will have been subjected to contestation and reinvention of the terms of the dialogue itself. If the possibility of recognizing the contingency of one's own socialization and pre-existing solidarities is built into the liberal cause itself then its morality cannot be placed beyond contingency. If, following Rawls, liberalism is necessarily "political" rather than "metaphysical," it will not matter in practice whether people accept liberal principles for their own sake or regard them as "merely" a prudent alternative. Weber would have expressed uneasiness whether we can so easily place ourselves beyond the dilemmas of theory presented in this study. This is perhaps why Rawlsian liberalism has occasioned a comunitarian response to liberalism which states that a deep conditioning of competence in matters of justice, or public morality, is itself the proper focus of politics rather than something that can remain secondary to "mutually advantageous cooperation." Rawls and others may argue that liberal democracy can be defended merely as an adaptation to modern developments but his call for a pre-emptive boundary between "ultimate" questions and political questions cannot remedy the tensions between theory and practice. As we have seen, Rorty believes "we" are the kind of people who need not look beyond "luck," the success of our social values, to justify our identification with liberal democratic public arrangements. But do we really want to become the kind of people for whom questions that are "too" important are fortunately not "especially" important to the openness and freedom that would characterize our political arrangements?

It is to Weber's credit that he did not adopt a policy of either Straussian esotericism or Rortyan therapeutic dismissal of "ultimate questions" in his discussions of the great issues of modern politics and culture, as well as the relation between theory and practice. He appeared to believe that the very point of intellectual activity is to make it hard for theorists to score easy political points or speak for those who have to make decisions. For Weber the developmental significance of both liberal democracy, as well as the "ethically neutral" institutions of bureaucratic capitalism, could not be assessed apart from one's judgement regarding the problems of the present. But the limits of objectivity do not require detachment from, or esoteric treatment of, the issues that preoccupy political and moral philosophers. The point of Weber's political thought was to offer a highly stylized interpretation of the forces of selection implied by the kinds of social constraints and options facing his society. The interplay of these forces were significant to him from the standpoint of their possible conditioning influence upon ethically relevant human qualities. In this sense Weber indeed did not separate questions of fact from questions of value. But he did break with those modern political theorists that try to purge ambiguity from the attempt to realize the substantive content of liberal democratic freedoms. Rousseau, and later theorists like Marx and Hegel, invited us to confront the paradox that freedom is alternatively the condition and result of an ethical life whose possibility is not programmed into us by nature. But they themselves evaded the ambiguous relationship between ethics and politics by presuming that the self-conditioning of society could itself become the equivalent to nature or an objective moral order.

By contrast Weber appreciated Nietzsche's insistence that if we are to gain distance from the contingencies that have determined who we are we must not pretend to place ourselves beyond contingency itself in the interpretation of this situation.[42] To risk one's identity means, in Nietzsche's own terms, that one can only adopt an ironic distance from the formation and maintenance of a given mode of solidarity or life-sustaining identity. But Weber rejected Nietzsche's apparent belief that this sphere of human struggle and contingency required a form of responsibility independent of politics if the tragic quality of existence is to be felt. Some contemporary theorists like Rorty and William Connolly have recognized the ways in which a liberal democratic politics might actually be enhanced by making room for the Nietzschean recognition of contingency. They show that although liberal democracy itself always invites morally ambiguous strategies of power in the realm

---

[42] Nietzsche, *Beyond Good and Evil: Prelude to a Philosophy of the Future*, p. 34.

of socialization and solidarity, it does so in such a way that we are always being challenged to determine which options and alternatives are more worthy of development than others. Indeed Weber believed that no moral ideal or 'truth' could control the very strategies of life and power by which it is conditioned or which it brings about. The line between morality and politics is necessary, but this is not an objection to liberalism. Indeed, not only the critics of liberalism, but also its staunchest defenders, acknowledge that no liberal community can be relieved of the burden of deciding which kind of distinction, type of equality among people or definition of freedom will matter most to it.

Weber believed that the attempt to endure the conflict of ideals residing in disparate spheres of culture represents the ongoing challenge of modernity. He therefore rejected the idea of a natural distinction, either within politics (Schmitt) or beyond it (Nietzsche), and he stopped short of re-interpreting everything worth struggling for from the perspective of a type of world in which morality would be placed in the service of life and power. However, Weber and Nietzsche usually had their eyes fixed on those problems of human existence that lay beyond the attempt to reconstruct, even pragmatically, our forms of moral socialization and solidarity. As a consequence they denied themselves the insight that liberal democracy may yet be valuable as an ethically significant means of adapting a society like ours to unique historical and political challenges. Those challenges and crises cannot exhaustively be comprehended only by intellectual and political interpretations that set out to confirm Nietzsche's statement that "morality has no value in itself." The concerns animating this statement may no longer require the same political conclusions. Perhaps they now animate our sense that our commitment to liberal democracy or "freedom and openness" in politics and society is meaningful, even though it cannot by itself provide assurance that the ultimate questions facing human beings receive the only kind of treatment they need. Indeed, as Max Weber intimated, it is we ourselves who decide whether the quality of our existence depends on something more than contingent "alternatives between values."[43]

---

[43] "The Meaning of 'Ethical Neutrality'," pp. 17–8.

Bibliography

Bibliographic citations are by book title when there is single authorship of the book even when chapters or selections were originally published as articles. Works are listed as articles or selections when appearing in a volume containing works by different authors. Titles of chapters originally published as articles or essays, or otherwise requiring special mention, are given primary designation over volume or book titles in footnotes.

ADORNO, THEODORE. *Negative Dialectics*. New York: Continuum Books, 1973.

ALBROW, MARTIN. *Max Weber's Construction of Social Theory*. Houndmills: Macmillan Education, 1990.

ALBERT, HANS. *Treatise on Critical Reason*. Translated by Amelie Rorty. Princeton: Princeton University Press, 1985.

ALEXANDER, JEFFREY. "Individuation and Domination." In *Max Weber: Rationality and Modernity*. London: George Allen and Unwin, 1989.

APEL, KARL-OTTO. *Towards a Transformation of Philosophy*. Translated by Glyn Adey and David Frisby. London: Routledge and Kegan Paul, 1980.

———. "The Problem of Philosophical Foundations in Light of a Transcendental Pragmatics of Language." In *After Philosophy: End or Transformation?* Edited by Kenneth Baynes, James Bohman and Thomas McCarthy. Cambridge, Mass.: MIT Press , 1987.

ARENDT, HANNAH. *The Human Condition*. Chicago: University of Chicago Press, 1958.

———. *On Revolution*, New York: Pelican Books, 1977.

ARISTOTLE. *Politics*. Translated by T.A. Sinclair. Middlesex: Penguin Books, 1964.

ARON, RAYMOND. *History Truth and Liberty*. Edited and Translated by Franciszek Draus. Chicago: University of Chicago Press, 1985.

BARKER, MARTIN. "Kant as a Problem for Weber." *British Journal of Sociology* 31 (1980):224-245.

BEETHAM, DAVID. *Max Weber and the Theory of Modern Politics*. Cambridge: Cambridge University Press, 1985.

BELL, DANIEL. *The Cultural Contradictions of Capitalism*. New York: Basic Books, 1976.

——. *The Winding Path*. New York: Basic Books, 1987.

BERNSTEIN, RICHARD. *The Restructuring of Social and Political Theory*. New York: Harcourt Brace Jovanovich, 1976.

——. *Philosophical Profiles*, Philadelphia: University of Pennsylvania Press, 1986.

——. *Beyond Objectivism and Relativism: Science, Hermeneutics and Praxis*. Philadelphia: University of Pennsylvania Press, 1983.

——. "Rorty's Liberal Utopia." *Social Research* 57 (1990):31–72.

BLOOM, ALLAN. *Giants and Dwarfs*. New York: Simon and Schuster, 1991.

——. *The Closing of the American Mind*. New York: Simon and Schuster, 1987.

BREINER, PETER. "Democratic Autonomy, Political Ethics and Moral Luck." *Political Theory* 17 (1989):550–74.

BRUBAKER, ROGERS. *The Limits of Rationality: An Essay on the Social and Moral Thought of Max Weber*. London: George Allen and Unwin, 1984.

CASTORIADIS, CORNELIUS. *Philosophy, Politics and Autonomy: Essays in Political Philosophy*. New York: Columbia University Press, 1991.

CONNOLLY, WILLIAM. *Identity \ Difference*. Ithaca: Cornell University Press, 1992.

DALLMAYER, FRED. *Critical Encounters: Between Philosophy and Politics*. Notre Dame: University of Notre Dame Press, 1987.

DEWEY, JOHN. *The Influence of Darwin on Philosophy and other Essays on Contemporary Thought*. New York: Holt, Rinehart and Winston, 1910.

——. *The Public and its Problems*. Chicago: Henry Holt & Co., 1927.

——. *Philosophy and Civilization*. New York: Minton, Balch and Co., 1931.

——. *The Philosophy of John Dewey*. Edited by John J. McDermott. Chicago: University of Chicago Press, 1973.

EDELMAN, MURRAY. *The Symbolic Uses of Politics*. Urbana: University of Illinois Press, 1964.

EDEN, ROBERT. *Political Leadership and Nihilism*. Tampa: University of Florida Press, 1983.

——. "Why Weber wasn't a Nihilist." In *The Crisis of Liberal Democracy: Straussian Perspective*. Edited by Kenneth Deutsche and Walter Soffer. Albany: SUNY Press, 1987.

FERRARA, ALESSANDRO. "A Critique of Habermas' *Diskursethik*." *Telos* 64 (1985):45–74.

FLEISCHMANN, EUGEN. "De Weber à Nietzsche." *Archives Européenes Sociologiques* 5 (1964):190–238.

FOUCAULT, MICHEL. *Discipline and Punish: The Birth of the Prison.* Translated by Alan Sheridan. New York: Viking Press, 1978.

———. "The Subject and Power." Afterword to *Michel Foucault: Beyond Structuralism and Hermeneutics* by Paul Rabinow and Hubert Dreyfuss. Chicago: University of Chicago Press, 1982.

GILBERT, ALAN. *Democratic Individuality.* Cambridge: Cambridge University Press, 1990.

GORDON, COLIN. "The Soul of the Citizen: Max Weber and Michel Foucault on Rationality and Government." In *Max Weber, Rationality and Modernity.* Edited by Sam Whimster and Scott Lash. London: Allen & Unwin, 1987.

HABERMAS, JÜRGEN. *Moral Consciousness and Communicative Action.* Cambridge, Mass.: MIT Press, 1990.

———. *The Theory of Communicative Action: Reason and the Rationalization of Society.* Vol. 1. Translated by Thomas McCarthy Boston: Beacon Press, 1984.

———. *The Theory of Communicative Action: System and Lifeworld.* Vol. 2. Translated by Thomas McCarthy. Boston: Beacon Press, 1987.

———. *Communication and the Evolution of Society.* Translated by Thomas McCarthy. Boston: Beacon Press, 1979.

———. *Legitimation Crisis.* Translation by Jeremy Shapiro. Boston: Beacon Press, 1975.

———. *The Philosophical Discourse of Modernity.* Cambridge Mass.: MIT Press, 1987.

———. *Toward a Rational Society.* Translated by Jeremy Shapiro. Boston: Beacon Press, 1970.

———. *Autonomy and Solidarity: Interviews with Jürgen Habermas.* Edited by Peter Dews. London: Verso Press, 1986.

———. "Justice and Solidarity: On the Discussion Concerning 'Stage 6'." *The Philosophical Forum* 21, nos. 1–2 (1989–90):32–52.

———. "Law and Morality," *Tanner Lectures on Ethics and Human Value.* Vol. 8. Salt Lake City: University of Utah Press, 1987.

HENNIS, WILHELM. *Max Weber: Essays in Reconstruction.* Translated by Keith Treib. London: Allen & Unwin, 1987.

JASPERS, KARL. *On Max Weber.* Translated by R.J. Whelan. Edited by John Dreijmanis. New York: Paragon House, 1989.

LARMORE, CHARLES. *Patterns of Moral Complexity*. Cambridge: Cambridge University Press, 1987.

LEVINE, DONALD N. *The Flight from Ambiguity*. Chicago: University of Chicago Press, 1985.

LINDBLOM, CHARLES. *Inquiry and Change: The Troubled Attempt to Understand and Change Society*. New Haven: Yale University Press, 1990.

LÖWITH, KARL. *Max Weber and Karl Marx*. London: Allen and Unwin, 1982.

LUHMANN, NIKLAS. *A Sociology of Law*. Translated by Martin Albrow and Ellen King. London: Routledge and Kegan Paul, 1985.

——. *The Differentiation of Society*. Translated by Stephen Holmes and Charles Larmore. New York: Columbia University Press, 1982.

——. *Political Theory in the Welfare State*. Translated by John Bednarz. Berlin: Walter de Gruyter, 1990.

LUKES, STEPHEN. "Of Gods and Demons." In *Habermas: Critical Debates*. Edited by John Thompson and David Held. Cambridge, Mass.: MIT Press, 1964.

MACINTYRE, ALISDAIRE. *After Virtue*. 2nd ed.. Notre Dame: University of Notre Dame Press, 1984.

——. *Whose Justice, Which Rationality?* Notre Dame: University of Notre Dame Press, 1988.

MARCUSE, HERBERT. *Negations*. Boston: Beacon Press, 1968.

——. *A Critique of Pure Tolerance* (with B. Moore and R.P. Wolff). Boston: Beacon Press, 1965.

MAYHEW, LEON. "In Defense of Modernity: Talcott Parsons and the Utilitarian Tradition." *American Journal of Sociology* 89 (1987):1273-305.

MCCARTHY, THOMAS. "A Response to Rorty's Reply." *Critical Inquiry* 16 (1990):644-71.

MERQUIOR, J.G. *Rousseau and Weber: Two Studies of the Theory of Legitimacy*. London: Routledge Kegan Paul, 1980.

MOMMSEN, WOLFGANG. *The Political and Social Theory of Max Weber*. Chicago: University of Chicago Press, 1989.

——. "Personal Conduct and Societal Change." In *Max Weber: Rationality and Modernity*. Edited by S. Whimster and S. Lash. London: Allen and Unwin, 1987.

——. "Max Weber and Roberto Michels." In *Max Weber and his Contemporaries*. London: Allen and Unwin, 1987.

NEHAMAS, ALEXANDER. *Nietzsche: Life as Literature*. Cambridge, Mass.: Harvard University Press, 1985.

NIETZSCHE, FRIEDRICH. *The Will to Power*. Translated by Walter Kaufman. New York: Vintage, 1967.

——. *The Gay Science*. Translated by Walter Kaufman. New York: Vintage, 1974.

——. *Beyond Good and Evil: Prelude to a Philosophy of the Future*. New York: Penguin, 1974.

OAKES, GUY. "Rickert's Value Theory and the Foundations of Weber's Methodology." *Sociological Theory* 61 (1988):38–51.

O'NEILL, JOHN. "Religion and Postmodernism: The Durkheimian Bond in Bell and Jameson." In *After the Future: Postmodern Times and Places*. Albany: SUNY Press, 1990.

PARSONS, TALCOTT. *Social Systems and the Evolution of Action Theory*. New York: Free Press, 1977.

——. *Politics and Social Structure*. New York: Free Press, 1969.

——. *On Institutions and Social Structure*. Edited by Leon Mayhew. Chicago: University of Chicago Press, 1982.

PATEMAN, CAROLE. *Participation and Democratic Theory*, Cambridge: Cambridge University Press, 1970.

POPPER, KARL. *The Poverty of Historicism*. New York: Harper & Row, 1944.

——. *Conjectures and Refutations*. London: Routledge and Kegan Paul, 1963.

PORTIS, EDWARD. *Max Weber and Political Commitment*. Philadelphia: Temple University Press, 1986.

RAWLS, JOHN. "Justice as Fairness: Political not Metaphysical." *Philosophy and Public Affairs* 14 (1985):223–51.

RAYNAUD, PHILLIPE. *Max Weber et les dilemmes de la raison moderne*. Paris: Presses Universitaires de France, 1987.

RORTY, RICHARD. *Contingency, Irony and Solidarity*. Cambridge: Cambridge University Press, 1989.

——. *Objectivism, Relativism and Truth*. Cambridge: Cambridge University Press, 1991.

——. *Essays on Heidegger and Others*, Cambridge: Cambridge University Press, 1991.

——. *Consequences of Pragmatism*. Minneapolis: University of Minnesota Press, 1982.

——. "Truth and Freedom: A Reply to Thomas McCarthy." *Critical Inquiry* (1990):633–43.

—— "Straussianism, Democracy and Allan Bloom," *The New Republic*, April 4, 1988, pp. 28–33.

ROSEN, STANLEY. "Leo Strauss and the Quarrel between the Ancients and the Moderns." In *Leo Strauss' Thought: Toward a Critical Engagement.* Edited by Adam Udoff. Boulder: University of Colorado Press, 1991.

ROUSSEAU, JEAN-JACQUES. *The Social Contract and Discourses.* Translated by G.D.H. Cole. London: Fitzhenry and Whiteside, 1973.

——. "Du bonheur public" (fragment), in *Oeuvres completes.* Vol. III. Paris: Gallimard, 1964.

SANDEL, MICHAEL. *Liberalism and the Limits of Justice.* Cambridge: Cambridge University Press, 1982.

SCAFF, LAWRENCE. "Politics in the Age of Subjectivist Culture: Weber's Thematic of the Modern." Paper delivered at American Political Science Association meetings, September 1987.

SCHELER, MAX. "Max Weber's Exclusion of Philosophy (On the Psychology and Sociology of Nominalist Thought)." In *Max Weber's Science as a Vocation.* Edited by P. Lassman and I. Velody. London: Allen and Unwin, 1988.

SCHLUCHTER, WOLFGANG and Guenther Roth. *Max Weber's Vision of History.* Berkeley: University of California Press, 1979.

——. *The Rise of Western Rationalism.* Berkeley: University of California Press, 1981.

SCHMITT, CARL. *The Concept of the Political.* Translated by George Schwab. Rahway: Rutgers University Press, 1976.

——. *The Crisis of Parliamentary Democracy.* Translated by Ellen Kennedy. Cambridge Mass.: MIT Press, 1985.

SMILEY, MARION. "Pragmatic Inquiry and Social Conflict: A Critical Reconstruction of Dewey's Model of Democracy." *Praxis International* 9 (1990):365–80.

STRAUSS, LEO. *Natural Right and History.* Chicago: University of Chicago Press, 1953.

——. *What is Political Philosophy and other Studies.* Chicago: University of Chicago Press, 1959.

——. *An Introduction to Political Philosophy.* Edited by Hilail Gildin. Detroit: Wayne State Press, 1989.

——. *The City and Man,* Chicago: University of Chicago Press, 1964.

———. "Relativism." In *Relativism and the Study of Man*. Edited by H. Schoek and J. Wiggens. Princeton: Van Nostrand, 1962.

———. "Social Science and Humanism." In *The State of the Social Sciences*. Edited by L. White. Chicago: University of Chicago Press, 1956.

———. "Political Philosophy and the Crisis of Our Time." In *The Predicament of Modern Politics*. Edited by Hermann Spaeth. Detroit: University of Detroit Press, 1964.

SUSSER, BERNARD. "Leo Strauss: The Ancient as Modern." *Political Studies* 36 (1988):497–514.

TAYLOR, CHARLES. *Hegel*. Cambridge University Press, Cambridge, 1975

TIRYAKIAN, EDWARD. *Sociologism and Existentialism*. Prentice Hall, Chicago, 1962

TODOROV, TZEVAN. "Le débat des valeurs: Weber - Strauss - Aron." *Information sur les Sciences Sociales* 25 (1986):53–65.

TURNER, BRYAN S. *Citizenship and Capitalism: The Debate over Reformism*. London: Allen & Unwin, 1986.

TURNER, CHARLES. *Modernity and Politics in the Work of Max Weber*. London: Routledge, 1992.

TURNER, STEPHEN and REGIS FACTOR *Max Weber and the Dispute over Reason and Value*. London: Routledge & Kegan Paul, 1984.

UNGER, ROBERTO. *Knowledge and Politics*. New York: The Free Press, 1975.

WALZER, MICHAEL. *Spheres of Justice: A Defense of Pluralism and Equality*. New York: Basic Books, 1983.

———. "A Critique of Philosophical Conversation." *The Philosophical Forum* 21 (1990):182–96.

———. "The Communitarian Critique of Liberalism." *Political Theory* 18 (1990):6–23.

———. "Liberalism and the Art of Separation." *Political Theory* 12, (1984):315–30.

WARREN, MARK. "Max Weber's Liberalism for a Nietzschean World," *American Political Science Review*, 82 (1988):31–50.

WEBER, MAX. *The Methodology of the Social Sciences*. Translated and Edited by Edward Shils and H. Finch, Glencoe: The Free Press, 1949.

———. *Economy and Society*. Vols. 1 and 2. Edited by Gunther Roth and Claus Wittich. Berkeley: University of California Press, 1978.

———. *Roscher and Knies: The Logical Problems of Historical Economics*. New York: The Free Press, 1975.

———. *Max Weber: The Interpretation of Social Reality*, New York: Schocken Books, 1971.

———. *From Max Weber: Essays in Sociology*. Translated and Edited by Hans. G. Gerth and C. Wright Mills. New York: The Free Press, 1946.

———. *The Protestant Ethic and the Spirit of Capitalism*. Translated by Talcott Parsons. New York: The Free Press, 1958.

———. *The Theory of Social and Economic Organization*. Translated and Edited by Talcott Parsons. New York: The Free Press, 1947.

———. *Weber: Selections in Translation*. Edited by W.G. Runciman. Translated by Eric Matthews. Cambridge: Cambridge University Press, 1978.

———. "Some Categories of Interpretive Sociology." *The Sociological Quarterly* 22 (1981):151–80.

———. *Max Weber On Universities: The Power of the State and the Dignity of the Academic Calling in Imperial Germany*. Translated and Edited by Edward Shils. Chicago: University of Chicago Press (Midway Reprint), 1973.

WILLIAMS, BERNARD. *Ethics and the Limits of Philosophy*. Cambridge: Harvard University Press, 1985.

WILSON, H.T. *The American Ideology*. London: Routledge & Kegan Paul, 1977.

———. *Political Management: Redefining the Public Sphere*. Berlin: Walter de Gruyter, 1985.

———. "Reading Max Weber: The Limits of Sociology." *Sociology* 10, (1976):297–315.

———. "Critical Theory's Critique of Social Science: Episodes in a Changing Problematic from Adorno to Habermas, Part II." *History of European Ideas* 7 (1986):287–302.

WOLIN, SHELDON. "Max Weber: Legitimation, Method and the Politics of Theory." *Political Theory* 9 (1981):401–24.

———. "Democracy in the Discourse of Postmodernism." *Social Research* 57 (1990):5–30.

Index

MAJOR CONCEPTS IN POLITICS AND POLITICAL THEORY

This series invites book manuscripts and proposals on major concepts in politics and political theory—justice, equality, virtue, rights, citizenship, power, sovereignty, property, liberty, etc.—in prominent traditions, periods, and thinkers.

Send manuscripts or proposals, with author's vitae to:

Garrett Ward Sheldon
General Editor
College Avenue
Clinch Valley College
University Virginia
Wise, VA 24293